Elizabeth and Philip

20 NOVEMBER 1947

Val Horsler

the national archives

First published in 2007 by

The National Archives
Kew, Richmond
Surrey, TW9 4DU, UK

www.nationalarchives.gov.uk

The National Archives brings together the Public Record Office,
Historical Manuscripts Commission, Office of Public Sector
Information and Her Majesty's Stationery Office.

A CIP catalogue record for this book is available
from the British Library.

ISBN 978 1 905615 23 0

Cover design, page design and typesetting by Goldust Design
Picture research by Gwen Campbell
Printed in Germany by
Bercker Graphischer Betrieb GmbH & Co

CONTENTS

INTRODUCTION
1947 – A Year of Extremes

For the people of Britain, the year 1947 began with the national emergency that was the bitterest winter for decades, and ended with a national celebration – the royal wedding of Her Royal Highness Princess Elizabeth and Lieutenant Philip Mountbatten. On the wedding day, Thursday, 20 November, the rain held off and there was little to dampen the enthusiasm of the thousands who thronged the centre of London to witness the processions. The country grasped the opportunity to fling their hats in the air, escape from everyday realities and feel good about themselves.

It was much needed. Truth to tell, there was rather less to feel good about in 1947 than the euphoria of Victory in Europe Day in 1945 had suggested there would be.

The Second World War was over, but international instability was coming from another quarter: the Iron Curtain was being drawn and the era of the US and Soviet superpowers squaring up against each other had begun. And the British Empire was becoming both unaffordable and increasingly untenable given the growing fervour for independence around the world. In a hugely symbolic act in August 1947, the British government hastily divested itself of the jewel in its imperial crown, India: 200 years of colonial history were wound up in a matter of only six months. Queen Victoria had gloried in her title as Empress of India. Her great-grandson, King George VI, now found himself having to relinquish the title, the final act overseen by Earl Mountbatten, uncle of his future son-in-law.

In Britain, winning the war had come at a price, not just in lives but also in a fractured landscape and a shattered economy. Two years on, the conflict still touched everybody, every day, in ways that were tangible and immediate. It was not just the piles of rubble everywhere, legacy of the bombing of the Blitz and the doodlebugs, but also the continued rationing – from meat and sweets to petrol – and the ever-present shortages. Moreover, the natural assumption that with every week that went by things would improve turned out to be unfounded: 1946 saw the rationing of bread, something that had not happened

1947
A country on rations

January
Winter weather causes new coal restrictions for homes and factories.

March
The fuel crisis becomes severe.

June
The milk allowance is reduced to 2½ pints (1 litre).

The government reduces train services by 10% compared with summer 1946.

Newspapers are limited to four pages.

September
Meat rations are cut.

Non-essential motoring is banned and restrictions imposed on travel abroad.

at all during the war years, and the restrictions in 1947 were even worse, partly because the year had begun with what seemed like a cruel blow from fate to add to the general misery – the coldest winter since 1883. Between January and March the country froze under feet of snow, 'icebergs' appeared in the North Sea, factories closed and the Labour Prime Minister, Clement Attlee, told the people to knuckle down for 'an emergency of the utmost gravity'.

Rationing had begun in January 1940, soon after the start of the war, and covered almost all necessities like food, petrol, clothes and furniture. With the coming of peace, people hoped that supplies would quickly get back to normal, but the economic legacy of such a devastating war meant that things got worse. In every family, each member received his or her own ration book with coupons for the weekly or fortnightly allowance. People were urged to dig up their gardens and every available plot of spare land to grow vegetables and the Ministry of Food issued regular advice on how to make the best of what little was available. However, even their upbeat slogan 'No end of delicious egg dishes with dried eggs' failed to convince the general public that dried eggs were nice to eat.

'PRINCESS IS TO WED'

Paris, Saturday.

THE Paris newspaper "France-Soir" stated to-day that Prince Philip of Greece will become a natural-ised British subject within six months and that six months afterwards, at the latest, his engagement to Princess Eliza-beth will be officially an-nounced.—B.U.P.

The Press Association Court correspondent writes:

On inquiry in London I was informed that there is nothing to add to the statement issued by Sir Alan Lascelles, private secre-tary to the King, some weeks ago. He then said that there was no truth in a report that Princess Elizabeth was engaged.

An article from the *Sunday Pictorial*, 1 December 1946.

Then in 1947, things got even tougher, with allowances further reduced and the misery heightened by the desperate shortage of fuel, exacerbated by the severe winter. There was a shortage of coal for homes and factories, and because petrol continued to be almost unobtainable, travel became difficult. An advertisement in *The Times* on the day of the royal wedding urged economy: 'We could save nearly a million tons between now and Christmas if we merely cut down our gas and electricity to what we used in 1938.'

Rationing was not to disappear completely until the 1950s; it applied to one and all, and the royal family was not exempt. It was against this background that Princess Elizabeth's wedding had to be planned.

When the royal engagement was announced, the government allowed Princess Elizabeth the extra 200 clothes coupons available to all brides. To top them up, women all over the country sent her their coupons as well – but it was illegal to pass on the coupons so they were all scrupulously sent back.

However, gifts from all over the world soon began flooding in to help with wedding preparations. Much of the material for the wedding dress came from abroad, and the ingredients for the wedding cakes were the gift of the Girl Guides of Australia. Home-made clothes and textiles arrived from home and abroad, as well as 131 pairs of nylons and 17 pairs of silk stockings. Of the 25 dresses the princess received as a gift from the New York Institute of Dress Designers, she kept five and, 'feeling that at this time of restrictions she could not keep all the dresses for herself', decided to give the other 20 to British girls who were being married that month, preferably to girls of her own age whose weddings were on 19, 20 or 21 November.

Gifts of food also came in, including 500 cases of tinned pineapple from the Governor of Queensland, Australia, and a box of apples from Kent. The Foreign Office files [FO 372] include a series of letters exchanged between the British Embassy in Washington DC and officials at home about the offer by an American organization called C.A.R.E. (Cooperation for American Remittances to Europe) to send, as a wedding present to the princess, food parcels for needy families. Much of the other largesse also was redistributed to worthy recipients, and the royal wedding breakfast itself was to reflect the austerity of the times: it consisted of three courses only.

Weather and the wedding

1947 was a spectacular year for weather. It started with one of the worst winters on record, in which the bitterly cold weather began in the middle of January and carried on right up until the middle of March. Ice floes were seen in the sea off Kent and blizzards cloaked the country in deep snow-drifts. Photographs show double-decker buses marooned in snow that reached their upper decks and people dwarfed by towering mountains of snow as they strode bravely along the roads.

In March, hurricane-force winds were recorded in some parts of southern England and rainfall in places was three times the average. As a result, the winter ended in massive flooding, particularly in York, Stratford-on-Avon, Tewkesbury and the Fens. However, the summer that followed turned out to be one of the hottest, according to records going back to the mid-17th century. Although there were severe thunderstorms in July, the next three months were warm and proved to be among the top ten driest autumns ever! Weather in England is unpredictable at the best of times, but in 1947 one did not know what to expect and the wedding day had to be planned for all eventualities.

There had been cold, wet weather in the days before the wedding, but fortune appeared to smile on London on 20 November when, as Frank Gillard of the BBC reported from his station outside Buckingham Palace just before the carriage processions were to start,

Freak weather

• In Kew, the sun shone for only 17 hours for the whole of February.

• In some places, the temperature fell to −21.3°C at night in late January.

• In early March, 20in (40cm) of snow fell in Birmingham in two days.

• Snowdrifts over 16ft (5m) high were reported in South Wales.

• In Oxford, temperatures were constantly below freezing from 10 to 26 February.

• In Surrey, about 120mm of rain fell in a few hours on 16 July.

• It was over 34°C on 3 June and was almost as hot on several days in August.

> The pavements are still damp but it is an hour since we have had rain. The temperature has gone up and it is almost a spring morning – such a relief to the enormous crowd which has been waiting for hours through the night and since before dawn.

As luck would have it, neither rain nor fog impinged on the pleasures of the day. All those who had waited out in the cold the night before and all those who joined them enjoyed an exhilarating day in, for once, surprisingly good autumn weather. Many stayed on the streets for hours, even into the evening when the newlyweds left the palace in an open landau for Waterloo Station. It was beginning to become misty then, and had also got very cold; but the royal couple were well wrapped up, with blankets over their knees covering discreet hot water bottles to help keep off the chill. As they set off on their new life together, the princess's corgi, Susan, tucked in at their feet, added her warmth as well.

Britain had experienced a difficult year, but finally it had its happy ending – all because, back in July 1939, a beautiful young English princess had met a dashing Greek prince and events had taken their course.

1

THE ENGAGEMENT
IS ANNOUNCED

After months of rumour and speculation, the royal romance was at last confirmed. To general delight, the Court Circular in *The Times* of 10 July 1947 carried the following announcement:

> BUCKINGHAM PALACE, July 9
> It is with the greatest pleasure that The King and Queen announce the betrothal of their dearly beloved daughter The Princess Elizabeth to Lieutenant Philip Mountbatten RN, son of the late Prince Andrew of Greece and Princess Andrew (Princess Alice of Battenberg), to which union The King has gladly given his consent.

A further formal announcement was carried in the Second Supplement to *The London Gazette* dated 31 July (plate 2), in order to satisfy the Royal Marriages Act of 1772. The Act declared that no member of the royal family under 25 might marry without the monarch's consent – and had to be obeyed. Elizabeth had convinced her father, however, and was now seen wearing her platinum and diamond

A telegram of congratulations from the government of Finland.

engagement ring. The extraordinary year was going to have a magnificent conclusion.

Before the announcement, of course, there had been months of diplomatic and procedural activity. This was no ordinary wedding – the Heiress Presumptive to the British throne had declared her intention to marry. And, although both Elizabeth and Philip were scions of European royalty (they were third cousins and great-great-grandchildren of Queen Victoria), their fortunes in life up to this point had been very different.

Princess Elizabeth Alexandra Mary, known to her close family as Lilibet, had been born on 21 April 1926, the first child of the Duke and Duchess of York. Her sister, Princess Margaret Rose, was born four years later. The family enjoyed the prosperous, sheltered, domestic life that suited Elizabeth's father Albert, known as 'Bertie', the second son of King George V. It came as a great shock when, less than a year after his flamboyant elder brother Edward became king in 1936, he abdicated from the throne to marry the divorcee Mrs Wallis Simpson. Not only was Bertie now faced with the burdens of kingship, but his elder daughter knew that in all likelihood she, too, would one day accede to the throne.

It is reported that, on the day Bertie left the family home as Duke of York to witness his brother's abdication and then returned home as King George VI, his two young daughters greeted him with deep curtseys. Their cosy, happy family life was to change radically. They went to live in huge, cold, draughty Buckingham Palace where they were at the centre of a working royal palace. The king and queen had increasingly busy lives, often away from home for months on end. There was more formality, more pageantry, less freedom; and, for Elizabeth at least, extra lessons on constitutional matters.

Philip's early life was very different. He was born in the family home in Corfu on 10 June 1921, the fifth child and the first son of Prince Andrew of Greece and his wife, Princess Alice of Battenberg. In fact, the family had not a drop of Greek blood; Philip's grandfather, the second son of King Christian IX of Denmark, had been offered the Greek throne as a young man, and had reigned for half a century. When a new republican government was formed in 1922, Philip's father, Prince Andrew, was arrested on charges relating to the recent disastrous Balkan war and found guilty. He was initially sentenced to death, but the sentence was soon commuted to lifetime banishment.

As a Prince of Greece and Denmark, briefly sixth in line to the Greek throne, Philip's future had looked promising. But now, when he was only 18 months old, the family had to flee. The British monarch, George V, came hastily to their rescue and sent a ship to take them off Corfu. Philip was carried aboard in an orange box and spent the rest of his life in exile from what might have been his homeland.

The family initially settled in France, but they were not to live together there for long. When Philip was only 10 his mother became ill and her son rarely saw her during his childhood. His father moved to Monte Carlo, where he died in 1944. His four sisters all married within 18 months, and went to live in Germany with their husbands. With his close family scattered, Philip's life now increasingly centred on Britain, where he was mostly educated. Although Philip had no permanent home at this point, he did have a large extended family with whom he could stay – although he was increasingly cut off from his sisters in Germany as war loomed – and a great deal of support from two uncles, Louis Mountbatten and George, Marquess of Milford Haven. His son David was Philip's

1947 *'We wish to congratulate ...'*

Telegrams and messages came in from far and wide.

Queen Elizabeth of the Belgians: 'Congratulations and good wishes.'

The Sultan of Morocco: 'Feelings of friendship.'

Juan Peron, President of Argentina and husband of Evita: 'My most sincere good wishes.'

The King of Afghanistan: 'The greatest pleasure.'

The Consul General of Basra, Iraq, on behalf of the British community: 'Warmest congratulations.'

The President of El Salvador: 'I share in the rejoicing.'

Pope Pius XII: 'Felicitations and the assurance of prayerful invocation of the choicest blessings.'

King Abdullah of Jordan: 'My great joy.'

High Chief Samuel A.K. Amalu of Hawaii: 'Best wishes for your betrothal.'

almost exact contemporary, close friend and later best man.

When Philip left Gordonstoun in 1939, he immediately joined the Royal Navy, and it was while he was a cadet at the Royal Naval College at Dartmouth that he first publicly met Princess Elizabeth. She was 13 years old and in Devon as part of a family trip on the Royal Yacht *Victoria and Albert*. He was requested to amuse the young princesses, and according to Marion Crawford, the princesses' governess, he showed off before her and 'Lilibet never took her eyes off him'.

They had come across each other several times before as they were both part of the extended European royal family, but this was their first formal meeting and the first during their growing-up, teenage years. Two photographs of the Dartmouth visit show them together: one where the two of them are playing croquet, and another in which he is enjoying a joke in the background with Louis Mountbatten while the royal family watch the cadets on parade. It is more than likely that the meeting had been engineered by the ambitious Mountbatten, who may have been trying to act as matchmaker between the future queen and his nephew. Whatever the circumstances, it was an undoubted success. Elizabeth was clearly smitten and Philip was openly delighted with his young distant relative. They kept in touch during the difficult war years when Philip was on active service with the Royal Navy; and it was probably the Christmas he spent with the royal family in 1943, when he and Elizabeth chatted and danced and had fun together, that cemented their burgeoning love.

The priority in those years, however, was the war. Philip spent most of the conflict in the Pacific, and for Elizabeth – aged 19 in 1945 when the war ended – there was a growing involvement

The Royal Coat of Arms as used by the monarch.

Elizabeth's war years

Sept 1939: Outbreak of Second World War. Elizabeth is 13. She and Margaret are based at Windsor Castle.

Oct 1940: Broadcasts on 'Children in Wartime' BBC series.

Feb 1945: Joins the Auxiliary Territorial Service (ATS) as No 230973 Second Subaltern Elizabeth Alexandra Mary Windsor. Attends classes on first aid and car mechanics and learns night driving.

with the business of royalty. She was 16 when she gained her first appointment as colonel of a guards regiment, and as Heiress Presumptive (not Heiress Apparent, in case her parents had a son who would supersede her), she sometimes deputized for her father when he was away visiting troops and she had to append the royal assent to Acts of Parliament. As the conflict drew to its close, she and her sister were able to enjoy a growing social life among suitable contemporaries; but it was clear to those close to her at the time that she had eyes and feelings for no one other than Philip. He too made good friends and had good times when he could, and he was later adamant that thoughts of marriage – with anyone – never entered his head while he was still actively involved in the war. Moreover, as peace descended he was able to spend time with his sisters in Germany, and he also saw his mother again when she travelled from Greece – where she had lived throughout the German occupation – to visit London. Although his father had died in France in 1944, with the war over Philip once again had his family.

At the same time it was clear to those around them that Elizabeth and Philip were falling in love. With her it had been instantaneous; he had grown into it gradually. But by the summer of 1946, while he was staying with the royal family at Balmoral, their feelings could no longer be denied; he proposed and she accepted. He was 25, she was 20.

Before the announcement

King George VI thought that his daughter was too young to marry. But she was determined, and all he could do was impose two conditions before he gave his consent. The first was that no public announcement of the engagement would take place before she turned 21 in April 1947; and the second was that there was to be a time for thought while the whole royal family went on a tour of southern Africa in the early part of that year.

They left towards the end of February, and thus missed the worst of that terrible winter. For Elizabeth, this first trip abroad was an eye-opener and an affirmation of her deep commitment to her destiny as the future queen of both Britain and the Commonwealth. It was while she was in

South Africa, on her 21st birthday on 21 April, that she made a broadcast to the whole of the British dominions. It contained the declaration that was to govern her royal life:

> I declare before you all that my whole life, whether it be long or short, shall be devoted to your service and the service of our great Imperial family to which we all belong. But I shall not have the strength to carry out this resolution alone unless you join in with me, as I now invite you to do.

The House of Commons logo.

Meanwhile at home, during the autumn of 1946 and the winter of 1946/7, behind-the-scenes machinations were preparing the way for the announcement of the royal engagement. Not the least of the issues was the question of Philip's status. He was now thoroughly Anglicized, but he was nevertheless a foreign national, a foreign prince and a member of the Greek Orthodox church. Moreover, his family had strong links with the country so recently at war with Britain; all four of his sisters had married into the German aristocracy, and some of their husbands had unfortunate connections. His position would have to be regularized before the royal family and the authorities could begin even to think about when and how to make the announcement.

Private Office documents [ADM 178/389] in the National Archives record the rumours that began in late November

1946, partly prompted by an article in the Paris newspaper, *France Soir*. It declared that Prince Philip of Greece would become a naturalized British subject within six months and then, six months later, his engagement to Princess Elizabeth would be officially announced. The report went on to say that Queen Elizabeth was in favour of the marriage, but that King George, while having the highest regard for Prince Philip, feared the political repercussions in Britain if the princess were to marry a foreigner so soon after the Second World War. It would therefore be essential for Prince Philip to become a naturalized Briton.

The story was widely repeated in the British press, and elicited a blunt denial from the Palace: 'There is nothing to add to the statement issued by Sir Alan Lascelles, private secretary to the king, some weeks ago. He then said that there was no truth in a report that Princess Elizabeth was engaged.'

However, a few days later in early December, the Home Secretary, Chuter Ede, had to field a question about Philip's naturalization in the House of Commons from George Jeger MP, who asked 'on what grounds priority is being given to his application?' The brief answer was that it was assumed that Prince Philip was seeking naturalization because he wished to remain in the Royal Navy. This approach had been agreed between the Home Secretary and the First Lord of the Admiralty, in consultation with Earl Mountbatten, in case the naturalization announcement might 'lead to a revival of the embarrassing rumours concerning Prince Philip and Princess Elizabeth' [ADM 178/389].

It is clear from the documents that timing was the issue here; there was no difficulty about Philip applying for and being granted British citizenship. He had served his adopted country well throughout the war, he had an exemplary naval record and he was precisely the sort of young officer the Royal Navy was anxious to retain. Many of his fellow 'aliens' in the armed forces were being granted citizenship easily and quickly. It was simply, in this case, a matter of the paperwork being processed at the right time, from the point of view of the palace and the government.

The palace did not wish Philip to become a British citizen until February or March 1947, to tie in with other arrangements being made for the engagement. Unfortunately, he had sent his application into the Admiralty in early December 1946, just as a quicker procedure was being adopted.

There followed a series of somewhat tortuous discussions between the Home Office and the Admiralty. Philip's application had already been widely reported in the press, so the authorities could not just sit on it until February or March. The procedure had been shortened and simplified to allow the many deserving candidates a faster track to British citizenship, and it was only those over whom a question mark hovered where applications took longer. As the naval member of the Board pointed out, if Philip's paperwork took several months to process, 'it might appear that there is some doubt about his suitability'.

It seemed that the only way to delay Philip's citizenship until February 1947 was for the Naturalization Board to revert to the longer and more costly procedure for all applicants. Despite the obvious inconvenience to both candidates and Board, this was what happened: the Home Office files record a note acknowledging receipt of Prince Philip's application for naturalization on 13 February 1947.

In due course, therefore, all went ahead as planned. In the middle of March 1947 Prince Philip of Greece and Denmark renounced his royal titles, was received into the Church of England and was accepted as a British citizen under the name

```
Princess Elizabeth's Engagement - Mr. Teofan
Liszniewicz.

        Encloses poem written by Mr.Liszniewicz.
Owing to the somewhat obscure style of the poem
it has not been found possible to submit a
coherent translation.
        Suitable acknowledgement has been sent
to the author.
```

The wry Foreign Office response to a poem sent to Elizabeth by a Polish poet.

Philip Mountbatten – an Anglicized version of his mother's name and that also borne by his uncle. From now until the day before the wedding he would be plain Lieutenant Mountbatten. Shortly after her 21st birthday, Elizabeth arrived back in Britain. The way was finally open for the announcement of their engagement four months later on 9 July, a date chosen because there was to be a garden party at Buckingham Palace on 10 July at which the newly engaged couple could make their first appearance together.

Congratulations

Thousands of congratulatory messages flooded into the palace after the announcement of the engagement and at the time of the wedding [FO 372]. Embassies abroad were deluged with messages too; the Copenhagen Embassy informed the Foreign Office that they were acknowledging them all but saw no need to pass them on. London replied, however, that Princess Elizabeth had 'expressed the hope that you will thank all those who send messages of congratulation, and that whenever possible the Ambassador will sign the letters of thanks himself.'

Among all the messages from heads of state came many from ordinary people who did not know Elizabeth or Philip but just wanted to express their good wishes. One of these was from 'a Swiss wireless repairer and his wife', and another came from Teofan Liszniewicz, who described himself as 'an impoverished Polish poet' and sent an impressively decorated sheet of parchment with a long, somewhat impenetrable poem in Polish. Less welcome was the letter from Andreas Fofolos of Athens who combined his good wishes with a request that the king might give a donation towards an Athenian church; the Foreign Office official who received this commented 'you may consider that his good wishes are therefore unworthy of acknowledgement'.

The inevitable questions of protocol came up. Messages from foreign royalty and some heads of state received replies from the king himself, like this one to Ibn Sa'ud, King of Saudi Arabia:

PRINCE PHILIP

To be British in a few weeks

Express Political Correspondent

AN application by Prince Philip of Greece for naturalisation as a British citizen will be approved "in a matter of weeks," it was stated in Whitehall last night.

An article from the *Daily Express*, 2 December 1946.

It has given me great pleasure to receive Your Majesty's kind greetings on the occasion of my daughter's betrothal and on behalf of Her Royal Highness I thank you most sincerely for the good wishes which you have expressed towards her at this happy time.

Vincent Auriol, President of France, similarly received a reply direct from the king, addressed to 'you and the people of our ally France', which added, 'It gives us especial pleasure that the French people should rejoice with us on

Philip's war years

1940: First posting as a midshipman.

1941: 'Mentioned in despatches' after Battle of Matapan; fights in Battle of Crete.

1942: Sub-lieutenant; served on HMS *Wallace*.

1943: Becomes first lieutenant.

1945: At Japanese surrender while serving on HMS *Whelp*.

this happy occasion.' Other replies were sent by the princess or, after the wedding, by both bride and groom. But some messages caused minor diplomatic flaps. It was regarded as inadvisable for the king to reply directly to the good wishes from King Zog and Queen Geraldine of Albania, now living in exile in Egypt, 'since there is a remote possibility that such a telegram might be used for propaganda purposes'. It was decided instead that the British Ambassador in Cairo should personally convey the king's thanks to the exiled monarch.

A similar conundrum faced the Prime Minister's office when he received a telegram from the Prime Minister of Greece, which referred to 'His Royal Highness Prince Philip'. Since Philip was, between the engagement and the wedding, no longer either a prince or HRH as far as the British authorities were concerned, the Foreign Office draft reply 'purposely omitted the name of the bridegroom' in case it might 'in Greek eyes, appear intentionally snubbing if we replied with reference to Lieutenant Mountbatten…'.

Greetings from President Soekawati of East Indonesia and the Bey of Tunis also prompted diplomatic flutterings. Was the President, officials asked, 'respectable enough to be made the recipient of an expression of thanks from Her Royal Highness?' It seems he was: the country had 'no international status but [was] respectable enough to merit an expression of thanks. This should however be done by the Consul General at Batavia at his discretion and in whatever manner he thinks best.' In the Bey's case, this was 'the first time the Bey had taken independent action in respect of an occasion concerning the head of a foreign state … though it will of course have been approved – if not suggested – by the French authorities and has in that light some political interest as a straw in the wind.'

It was greetings from members of the Japanese royal family that caused the greatest consternation (plate 10). The British

Embassy in Tokyo had managed to deflect official congratulations from Emperor Hirohito and from the Japanese Prime Minister, which would not have been at all appropriate 'given the state of war which legally exists between the two countries', but private good wishes sent by two of the Japanese princes still had to be dealt with. In order to avoid publicity and leave no paper trail, thanks

Official Coat of Arms as used by the government.

would be transmitted orally by the Ambassador to Princes Takamatsu and Chichibu and their wives.

Settling the Civil List

Financial arrangements for the royal family, through the Civil List, were a matter for Parliament, and this was the first occasion in modern times that provision would have to be made for an Heiress Presumptive to the British throne who was about to marry. Queen Victoria had married after her accession to the throne, and all Heirs Apparent since had been entitled to the substantial revenues of the Duchy of Cornwall. There was thus some debate in cabinet, and through a select committee, as to how the princess and her future husband were to be provided for.

There were two issues: the first was the prevailing austerity, under which it was felt that too generous a provision could not be countenanced, particularly under a Labour government; and the second was the lack of precedent for what would clearly be the increased needs of a grown-up, married Heiress Presumptive and her consort.

The beautifully handwritten minutes of cabinet meetings in the autumn of 1947 [CAB 195/5] record the debate about the necessary increase in the provision for Princess Elizabeth and her husband. She was receiving £15,000 a year tax-free, and the broadest estimates of her future needs provided for a figure of £60,000 a year, of which £10,000 was to be for Philip. The cabinet, however, felt that 'although these sums are not high on a comparison with the sums which have been authorized by Parliament in the past, it would be difficult to justify such high figures at the present time.' Therefore the initial suggestion was to raise Princess Elizabeth's £15,000 to £30,000 and to pay £10,000 of that to Philip.

Later select committee discussions raised the overall figure to £40,000; but in the event the king himself came to the rescue. He suggested that the increase in his daughter's provision and the new allowance for her husband need not be a charge on the public purse, but could be funded from the surplus built up in his own allowance because of the decrease in ceremonial activities during the war, along with personal economies made by the royal family. It was calculated that these funds would cover Elizabeth's and Philip's needs for the next two years, after which the matter could be raised again. But even so there were some grumblings around the cabinet table: 'There is a feeling in the Labour Party that this is not the proper time for this [increase]'; and 'Our people will ask – is HM entitled to this surplus?' But the general feeling in cabinet was that 'if we have a royal family, we must keep it in proper state'. The House of Commons clearly agreed: when the king's offer was made known to the House in the days before the wedding, it was greeted with cheers and acclamation.

The invitations

Amidst all the practical preparations for the wedding, protocol had to be satisfied too. The guest list for the abbey was to include members of royal families from all over Europe; but there could clearly be no invitations extended to those with connections to countries recently at war with Great Britain. This prohibition meant that Philip's three surviving sisters, married to German aristocrats, could not be invited to their regret. There was no such difficulty with his mother, Princess Andrew, who had been born in Britain, at Windsor Castle, and had undertaken charitable work in Greece during the war. After the wedding, she consoled her daughters for their enforced absence by writing a 22-page description of the day for their benefit.

The cabinet also debated whether an invitation could be issued to the king's cousin, a Spanish nobleman, in the light

The princess's rings

Engagement ring: platinum and a large central diamond, smaller stones at either side. The diamonds came from a tiara belonging to Princess Andrew, who commissioned the ring from a Bond Street jeweller, since Philip could not appear personally at a jeweller's for that purpose.

Wedding ring: fashioned from the nugget of Welsh gold that had been given to Elizabeth's mother for her own ring.

of relations with the Franco regime; in the event they raised no objections. However, the most notable absentees from the guest list were Princess Elizabeth's uncle and aunt, the Duke and Duchess of Windsor, who had been almost completely estranged from the royal family since his abdication from the throne in 1936. As the *Daily Mirror* was to report on 21 November, the couple were in New York on the day of the wedding, and refused to make any comment on the occasion to the American press, saying that it was a family matter. The Duke of Windsor's sister, Princess Mary, the Princess Royal, was another senior member of the family who did not attend, ostensibly because of ill health.

George VI invented the expression 'the family firm' about the House of Windsor. That 'firm' and all its aides had swung into action to smooth out all the wrinkles and knots that were an inevitable part of the plans for a royal wedding. All those who plan weddings know how tortuous the arrangements can be; and this family had to cope not only with the protocol and diplomacy that are a central part of royalty, but also with a ceremony that was to take place amidst austerity and hardship. Alongside all the work in progress behind the palace walls, officials in Whitehall, as well as at Westminster Abbey, were deeply embroiled with the preparations for the ceremony and the processions. It was truly to be an unforgettable day.

2

PLANS AND PREPARATIONS

The engagement immediately instigated a flurry of activity in the Ministry of Works, the Home Office and the Metropolitan Police. These government departments were responsible, in conjunction with the authorities of Westminster Abbey, for the practical arrangements for the wedding, and the legacy of their efforts graces the files of the National Archives [AE 9012/1, HO 144/23364 and MEPO 2/7967 respectively]. We now meet R. Auriol Barker of the Ministry of Works, one of the many officials who would work indefatigably over the next few months to ensure that everything went smoothly. No detail was too small for Mr Barker's attention, but he was having to contend not only with the time allowed to him – the wedding was to take place on 20 November, a mere four months away – but also with the prevailing shortages at this time.

Barker's first memo precisely pointed out these problems. He swiftly discounted any possibility of floodlighting Buckingham Palace because of fuel shortages (though in the end it was agreed that floodlighting could be allowed, for two nights only, 19 and 20 November), and could not contemplate lining the Mall with flagpoles, though he would place some in front of the palace. Fireworks, however, he thought, would be a good idea and also cheap and easy, because the explosive chemicals used in them 'are, I believe, in abundant supply as being a war surplus'. Green Park would be the best venue for a firework display, Barker suggested, because it was close to the palace, 'provided arrangements can be made for a sufficiently large area to receive the falling sticks'.

The Lord Chamberlain's Office, under the Earl of Clarendon, handled the arrangements from Buckingham Palace's perspective, and appears to have been all too aware of the path to be trodden between the desire for a great celebration and the country's current struggles. Although there would be large numbers of guests invited to the ceremony – Barker reported that he could easily provide seating for 2,600 guests on the floor of the abbey – there were to be no stands erected outside the abbey or along the route, even though the Canadians made a generous offer of timber for their construction. The only stands would be for the press, although one within the abbey would

The logo of the Royal Mews Department, Buckingham Palace.

> **Royal wedding venues**
>
> Chapel Royal, St James's Palace: Queen Victoria and Prince
> Albert (1840); Edward VII (then Prince of Wales) and
> Alexandra of Denmark (1863); George V (then Duke of York)
> and Mary of Teck (1893).
>
> Westminster Abbey: George VI (then Albert, Duke of York)
> and Elizabeth Bowes Lyon (1923); Elizabeth II (then Princess
> Elizabeth) and Philip (1947).

also be for the use of the clergy who would be unable to
occupy their usual seats in the choir. This stand was later to
cause friction between the Ministry and the abbey's Dean
and Chapter, when the Chapter Clerk was billed £92 for
their share of the costs of it. As the Dean pointed out, accommodation in the stands was in compensation for the loss of
seats in the choir, and he didn't see why they had to pay. But,
as he grumpily agreed, it was by then too late to argue.

War damage, too, was a factor that had to be taken into
account. The abbey's Chapter House had been badly hit,
with much of its medieval stained glass shattered; but it was
regarded as an ideal cloakroom for the Gentlemen-at-Arms,
so the broken glass, awaiting conservation and reinstate-
ment, would have to be removed and a cover provided to
protect the rare medieval tiled floor. Along the route of the

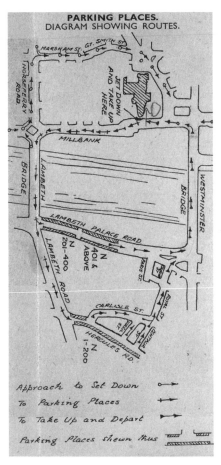

PARKING PLACES.
DIAGRAM SHOWING ROUTES.

Approach to Set Down ○——
To Parking Places ——
To Take Up and Depart ▶▶▶
Parking Places shewn thus

Diagram showing route to parking places.

processions, a number of bombed-out buildings would have to be securely boarded up so that they could not be used as vantage points in their unsafe condition. One of these was 2 Carlton Gardens, next door to the Foreign Secretary's residence, where many invited guests would be viewing the events; the resident warden would have to be supplemented by additional safety works in case the guests were tempted to spill over.

It was also clear that some unprecedented arrangements would have to be made for the BBC, who were broadcasting the service on the radio and – for the first time – televising the processions between the palace and the abbey. The triforium, a gallery above the nave, was to be set aside for the BBC's use, with the provision of two sound-proof booths there. They were also allowed to position a TV van in Little Sanctuary, outside the abbey. The space allocated to them there was increased in early November because they had just acquired a new camera which would allow them to get better pictures in the sort of poor lighting conditions that might be expected on 20 November.

In the event, the BBC had to share their accommodation in the triforium with 88 members of Buckingham Palace staff, who had been issued with tickets to witness the service from this vantage point. There was some worry that 'because the view is restricted from some of the positions … they may climb about to obtain a better view and so endanger themselves and the congregation on the floor of the abbey which is a considerable distance below.' A police officer would therefore be posted there to stop any such dangerous activity.

Barker kept a strict eye on the costs. The carpets and awnings caused a certain amount of tension between those variously involved. The police came up with an elaborate scheme of awnings at all the abbey entrances, but Barker regarded this as both inessential and far too expensive. He also pointed out that he could not offer a red carpet, but could provide a new blue one along with a stone-coloured felt drugget to run along its edges. The abbey, however, had already asked one of their suppliers, B. Edginton & Co., to furnish them with a carpet, and Edginton's confirmed that they did indeed have a red one, albeit not new. The widths of the two possible carpets were another matter for discussion; the blue one was wider, so guests would have to walk on it and would maybe get it muddy. Costs also varied, and it was only after much to-ing and fro-ing that agreement was reached on the red carpet and the stone-coloured drugget.

Lieutenant Mountbatten's lack of formal status during the planning stages was a headache for Barker, in that it was unclear what cipher should be used on the flags and banners. Since the Lord Chamberlain's Office

> knew nothing of any proposals regarding the arms or titles projected for Lieutenant Mountbatten… in the circumstances there seems nothing for us to do but to make use of the ciphers E and P separately or entwined. [AE 9012/1]

By early September it had been agreed that flags would be hung in Whitehall and masts for flags erected in front of Buckingham Palace, but the question of floodlighting the palace was still under discussion. Coal and fuel were at such a premium that it was unclear whether the advantage to the gaiety of the occasion could be balanced with what might be seen as a waste of resources. It was not until 9 October that the Ministry of Fuel and Power finally sanctioned the cost.

Even the colour of the window boxes along the processional route was a matter for detailed consideration, along

Parking plans on the wedding day

This was the order of parking in Dean's Yard ready for the return from
Westminster Abbey to Buckingham Palace, as detailed by the police:

A	1 motor car	Sir Piers Legh (Master of the Household) and other palace officials
B	1 Ford van	King's valet and two dressers
C	1 motor car	Superintendent Royal Mews
D	2 outriders 1 coach	Bride and Bridegroom
E	1 royal car 4 motor cars	Bridesmaids, grooms, pages
F	2 outriders 1 coach 5 carriages	Their Majesties and other royalty and suites
G	1 royal car	The Crown Equerry
H	5 motor cars	Queen Mary, foreign royalty Other royalty and suites

with what could be planted in them to brighten up a possibly
drab November day:

Because the season is late the display will depend on foliage.
For this purpose the boxes would preferably be cream, but
since dark green is better in the long term perhaps they
could be painted cream in situ before being removed after

The logo of the
Metropolitan Police.

the wedding and repainted green prior to being replaced in the spring. [AE 9082/1]

Civil servants at the Ministry of Health had asked for the plants to be in pots within the window boxes so that they could be removed and not interrupt the view. Those working in government departments along Whitehall would clearly be in a privileged position when it came to viewing the processions, but the documents hint at some tension here, too. On 12 November, a question in Parliament to the Prime Minister asked 'which ministers have given instructions that civil servants on the royal wedding route are not to view the procession from the windows, and why?' The Prime Minister answered, 'None, sir, that I know of.' Princess Elizabeth's wedding day was not a public holiday, and workers would be expected to turn up as usual, but it was clear that, while the processions and the service were going on, interest and excitement would get in the way of the normal working day for most of those whose workplace would give them a view of the proceedings.

The spectators

The Members of Parliament and their guests traditionally enjoyed exclusive use of the pavement by New Palace Yard on these sorts of occasions, and were accorded the same privilege this time. But when they asked if they could also have exclusive access to the east side of Parliament Square Green, their request was denied; in addition, as a police instruction enjoined, 'It is strictly forbidden for anyone to view the procession from the roofs of the Palace of Westminster.' Parliamentary staff were issued tickets for the pavement on the south side of Parliament Square, and the boys of Westminster School were also allowed a vantage point within the abbey railings; it was even noted that they might climb on to the Crimea memorial, if necessary. But when the awnings went up, it became clear that their view would be obstructed, so they were given a position on the south pavement of the Sanctuary, with the injunction to the headmaster, 'You will doubtless ensure that the boys remain on the pavement and do not encroach into the roadway.'

A student rag

On 19 November a policeman travelling on a bus in London overheard 'two young men of the student type' talking about 'the fellows at King's College having a "rag" in town tomorrow' (plate 5). The youths joked that they would present Princess Elizabeth with their mascot Phineas – prompting the diligent officer to report it to the authorities. Even he agreed, however, that 'political motivation' did not seem to be a threat.

The Metropolitan Police were also engaged in some correspondence with the council of the church of St Margaret's which, owing to its proximity to Westminster Abbey, 'were contemplating offering tickets for sale to the public to enable them to stand in the churchyard to view the royal wedding processions.' It seemed that in the past the church had 'relied a great deal on the income received from the sale of seats during large functions.' They accepted that the erection of stands was out of the question this time, but they were nevertheless reluctant to forego the revenue. However, the tenor of the times was against this initiative, and they soon dropped the idea of selling tickets; instead they issued passes to members of the church, and arranged to bring benches out into the churchyard so that they could stand on them and get a good view. They were however warned that 'all spectators must be in position by 9am'.

English lion and Scottish unicorn on the Royal Arms.

The documents hint that the police did not always know what the Lord Chamberlain's Office was doing about special arrangements for specific parties of spectators. Memos received by the police simply 'informed' them that areas of pavement in front of Buckingham Palace had been allocated to 'approximately 600 schoolchildren' and 'a party of Girl Guides not exceeding 100', and they were asked to 'make the necessary arrangements'. The list of parties given privileged access to the pavement outside the palace does appear to be a little haphazard. The Girl Guides' presence is understandable – the palace had established its own company for the benefit of the princesses – as are the places allocated to 50 members of Norman Hartnell's staff. And a party of disabled trainees from Queen Elizabeth's Training College for the Disabled in Leatherhead, who would be 'arriving by coach at about 8.15am and setting down as near as possible to the palace forecourt', might also expect to receive special consideration. But one wonders why two particular schools were included out of all those who might have applied, and why, specifically, a youth centre from Preston and a street party from the Old Kent Road were given priority. Perhaps it simply was 'first come, first served'.

Other than those with access to good viewpoints, the vast crowds that were expected to line the roads would have to make the best they could of devices such as cardboard periscopes, or arrange to arrive early and brave the weather to establish a claim to a good position.

Security issues

Special Branch officers had visited all premises on the line of the route to ensure that buildings overlooking the procession would be either securely locked or open to authorized people only. Where observation points had been let, checks were being made on those who had been allocated places. The sewers under the route were searched on the morning of the wedding, and one Special Branch officer was to report to the suitably titled 'Inspector of Flushing' that morning, and then accompany the staff doing the search. Sand-boxes, lamp standards and 'a disused paraffin store situated under the roadway in Whitehall, opposite Downing Street' would also be searched. Road gullies would be flushed through. Telephone, water and electricity inspection covers would be lifted and checked. The London Underground also needed inspection, because the District Railway runs under the line of the route between Westminster and St James's Park stations, and the roof of the tunnel near Parliament Sqaure is less than 4ft below the road surface.

There was also a panic just days before the wedding when staff at the Savoy Hotel went on strike after the dismissal of a waiter (page 54). Amid fears that the waiter may have been a Communist spy planted to foment unrest and disrupt the wedding – the problem was even discussed at cabinet level – the police were alerted to expect trouble. But in the event there was no disruption.

Bomb-damaged premises were to be secured against would-be spectators climbing in. Premises along the route not occupied by government offices were to be visited to ensure security, among them the French Embassy, the Savage, Union and Crockford's Clubs and Colonel Astor's residence. Building sites on the route were to be searched, and access for workmen, whose names were being checked by Special Branch, would be through restricted entrances on the day; essential post-war reconstruction work would continue as usual. Officers were to be stationed on the press stands and on roofs and balconies. Access points would be manned and passes issued to those authorized to use them.

Westminster Council decided that public lavatories would be kept open for extended hours, even if others further away had to be closed to allow the staff to transfer. It was pointed out that the route on this occasion was much shorter than that of the Victory Parade in 1946, which made for greater vigilance since there would be a heavier concentration of spectators. On the other hand, the coffee stall run by Mrs Rosina Stratton in Broad Sanctuary, close to the abbey, was to be closed that day, at least until 'abnormal traffic' had departed. The police had originally wanted

Royal guests

Princess Andrew of
  Greece
Prince Regent of Belgium
King of Iraq
Queen of Roumania and
  the Duchess of Aosta
King and Queen of
  Yugoslavia
Prince and Princess
  George of Greece
Princess Christopher
  of Greece
Duchess of Kent
Princess Alice, the Earl
  of Athlone and Lady
  Helena Gibbs
Queen of Spain
Prince and Princess
  René of Bourbon
  Parma
Princess Axel of Denmark
Prince John and
  Princess Elizabeth of
  Luxemburg
Earl and Countess
  Mountbatten

43

the stall to be moved, but when she pointed out that this would mean the disconnection of the electricity supply, at a probable cost of around £10, they agreed that she should close it instead 'on the clear understanding that you alone will be responsible if any damage were to be caused to your stall by the presence of the crowd.'

Despite all this security, an extraordinary breach occurred on the day of the wedding within Westminster Abbey itself. A Mrs Wilcox had somehow managed to get into a position inside the abbey from which she could have almost touched the bride as she and her new husband walked down the aisle (plate 17). The authorities immediately made enquiries, and it turned out that she had been standing, as a guest of the Dean, on the roof of the Deanery overlooking the West Door, when she had felt cold and decided to go inside. Apparently she was then able to pass, without being challenged, through St George's Chapel and right to the West

The letterhead of the P & O Company who lent their offices for a police canteen.

Door; moreover – according to the Chapter Clerk, Mr Hebron – 'as far as the abbey authorities were concerned there was no objection to this.' The police made a statement that would undoubtedly be impossible today: 'The Commissioner is satisfied … that the precautions taken on this occasion by both the abbey and police authorities were entirely satisfactory.'

Mandarins and merchandise

Government officials greeted the arrival of various requests from canny entrepreneurs to manufacture souvenir items bearing the royal image or the royal arms with some surprise and befuddlement. A healthy debate followed, gravely monitored in memos concerning the advisability – or otherwise – of permitting such and such an item to be developed [HO 144/23364]. The general view was that it was Not a Good Thing.

The decision was taken, only days after the royal engagement, not to issue a general announcement about souvenirs, although Commander D. Colles of the Privy Purse, realizing that such things could not be formally prevented, deemed it advisable that the authorities should at least 'give an

In which we serve

Courtiers:
John 'Jock' Colville, Elizabeth's private secretary.
Lady Alice Egerton, a lady-in-waiting.

Domestic:
Margaret 'Bobo' Mac-Donald, Elizabeth's dresser and lifelong companion.
John Dean, Philip's valet who, like Bobo, accompanied the couple on honeymoon.

indication of what good taste would permit'. Home Office officials, however, obviously hoped that the economic situation would deter manufacturers from these ventures; H.S. Strutt of the Home Office, clearly underestimating the British capacity to spot a commercial opportunity, declared in a memo on 15 July:

> There are so many domestic needs to be satisfied which are a long way from satisfaction that it seems to me doubtful whether industry generally, in its various branches, would be able to venture into the field of permanent souvenirs, even if it wanted to and had the necessary materials available.
>
> [HO 144/23364]

Nevertheless, some intrepid manufacturers decided to go ahead, and Colles produced a template letter offering terms for souvenir makers: the items had to be on sale before the wedding and off sale three months afterwards. The indefatigable Strutt suggested a ruse whereby he would respond to requests for permission with the formula 'the suggestion is not one for which formal permission can be given', and 'leave the firm to draw its own conclusion'. In other words, he planned to adopt a deliberately ambiguous form of words that he hoped would be taken as a refusal, when in fact no formal permission was needed.

The Home Office's H. Dodd dealt with the Cheadle Fabric Co., who wished to produce handkerchiefs 'bearing reproductions' of Elizabeth and Philip. Dodd replied that 'where a handkerchief would, by virtue of its small size, design and material, not be suitable for the ordinary purpose for which handkerchiefs are made, but would be purchased and laid away as a souvenir of an historic occasion, objection would not be taken.' Fine, therefore, to produce souvenir handkerchiefs – just so long as their purchasers were unlikely to blow their noses on them!

Not all requests met with disapproval. The same Mr Dodd described a cut glass vase, submitted by Stourbridge Cut Glass and Tableware, as 'of very nice workmanship … towards the top of which appeared a six-arched and highly fanciful crown that by no stretch of the imagination could be said to resemble the Royal Crown.' The firm was told that the Secretary of State had no objection to the vase.

Another request came from Charles Hillingdon & Co., who wished to produce a commemorative brooch bearing not the royal arms themselves, but images resembling them. The company pleaded that there were precedents in the items manufactured for the coronation of George VI. But its representative was outwitted by Mr Storr, a nimble-footed official who noted: 'I was, fortunately, able to tell him that at the time of the Coronation I was not in England and had therefore not seen the objects to which he referred.' Hillingdon retreated. But they needn't have felt too bad, as even the BBC was frustrated in its attempt to use the princess's arms for the *Radio Times* that week.

Perhaps the Home Office would have happily settled for the brooch if it had come to a choice between that and the gruesome plastic flag that the Crescent Studio wanted to produce for the wedding day (page 52). As there was nothing they could do to stop it, Storr's letter to the company managed to combine brisk efficiency with barely concealed contempt:

A.1.

The following is an extract from our letter to The Controller, M.P.F.S, dated 31st October, 1947, and mentioned at "A" of the attached letter from The Controller.

Canteen	No. of men to be served.
1. Wellington Barracks (mobile canteen)	325
2. St. James's Park, by Artillery Memorial (marquee)	900
3. Spring Gardens, south side, (mobile canteen)	325
4. Green Park, by Canada Gates (marquee)	1,200
5. P. & O. Offices, Cockspur Street	350
6. Great Scotland Yard	700
7. Cannon Row Police Station	1,100
8. Central Hall, Princes Street, Westminster	1,100
Total	6,000

A memorandum setting out catering arrangements for the police.

1 The engaged couple – Princess Elizabeth and Lieutenant Philip Mountbatten step confidently forward as plans for their wedding start to gather pace.

3589

SECOND SUPPLEMENT

TO

The London Gazette

Of TUESDAY, the 29th of JULY, 1947

Published by Authority

Registered as a newspaper

THURSDAY, 31 JULY, 1947

At the Court at *Buckingham Palace*, the 31st day of *July*, 1947.

PRESENT

THE KING'S MOST EXCELLENT MAJESTY.

HIS ROYAL HIGHNESS THE DUKE OF GLOUCESTER.

> Archbishop of Canterbury.
> Lord Chancellor.
> Prime Minister.
> Lord President.
> Viscount Addison.
> Mr. Secretary Ede.
> Mr. Churchill.

Mr. Howe, Minister of Reconstruction and Supply, Canada.
Mr. Beasley, High Commissioner for the Commonwealth of Australia.
Mr. Jordan, High Commissioner for the Dominion of New Zealand.
Mr. Stratford, former Chief Justice of the Union of South Africa.
Sir Alan Lascelles.

His Majesty was this day pleased, in pursuance of the Royal Marriages Act, 1772, to declare His Consent to a Contract of Matrimony between His Most Dearly Beloved Daughter The Princess Elizabeth Alexandra Mary and Lieutenant Philip Mountbatten, R.N., son of His late Royal Highness Prince Andrew of Greece, G.C.V.O., and of Her Royal Highness Princess Andrew, R.R.C., which Consent His Majesty has caused to be signified under the Great Seal and to be entered in the Books of the Privy Council.

E. C. E. Leadbitter.

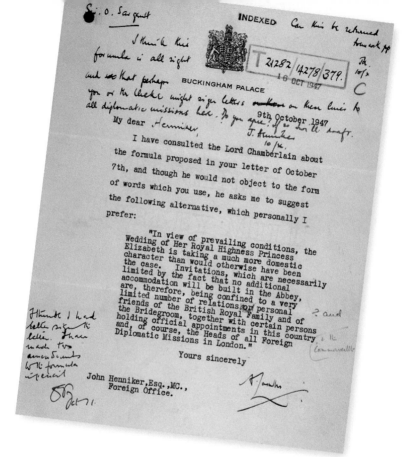

S. O. Sargent

INDEXED   Can this be returned
                    from work pp

I think this
formula is all right   [crest]
and so that perhaps   T 21282/14278/379.
                                    16 OCT 1947
BUCKINGHAM PALACE
you or the clerks might sign letters ~~on~~ on these lines to
all diplomatic missions here. Do you agree? If so send the draft.
                                                9th October 1947
                                                J. Henniker
My dear Henniker,   10/16.

I have consulted the Lord Chamberlain about
the formula proposed in your letter of October
7th, and though he would not object to the form
of words which you use, he asks me to suggest
the following alternative, which personally I
prefer:

"In view of prevailing conditions, the
Wedding of Her Royal Highness Princess
Elizabeth is taking a much more domestic
character than would otherwise have been
the case. Invitations, which are necessarily
limited by the fact that no additional
accommodation will be built in the Abbey,
are, therefore, being confined to a very
limited number of relations or personal
friends of the British Royal Family and of
the Bridegroom, together with certain persons   2 and
holding official appointments in this country,
and, of course, the Heads of all Foreign   + the
Diplomatic Missions in London."   Commonwealth

                            Yours sincerely

I think I had
better sign the
letter. I have
made two
amendments
to the formula
in pencil   John Henniker,Esq.,MC.,
                    Foreign Office.
8 Oct 1.

2 *Opposite:* The official announcement of the royal engagement in the Second Supplement to *The London Gazette*, 31 July 1947 (WORK 21/254). The formal notice was issued in accordance with the Royal Marriages Act, 1772.

3 *Above:* Tact and care were needed in responding to enquiries from abroad about wedding invitations as many had to be disappointed. The agreed wording stressed the 'domestic character' of the wedding to soften the blow (FO 372/6087).

4 Three young women brave the cold autumn night with groundsheets and blankets in order to secure a good position for the wedding.

5 *Left:* Concerns about security were never far from the surface. This report of a possible prank by King's College students on the wedding day was made by a policeman who overheard them discussing the idea on a bus (MEPO 2/ 7967).

6 *Opposite:* Prepared as ever, the Boy Scouts Association agreed to supply 40 Rover Scouts as messengers (MEPO 2/ 7967).

Metropolitan Police　　R.d/88L　　No. 730.

Reference { C.O. ⎰ to Papers { Divl. ⎱　　Blackheath Road　　STATION.　"R"　DIVN.

20th November　　194 7 :

30C

S.D.Inspector,

On 19.11.47. at 9.25pm whilst travelling to Blackheath Road for duty, as two young men of the student type were leaving the bus, I overheard **one** remark something to the effect 'that the fellows at King's College were having a 'rag'in town to-morrow and that they were going to make a presentation to Princess Elizabeth of their mascot, 'Phineas'. The remark was made in a jovial manner and there did not appear to be any apparent political motive. I was unable to confirm if there was any substance in the remark, but on reflecting on the recent escapades of the London Colleges, I treated the available information on its merits and informed A.2. and Special Branch accordingly. Message No.3 attached.

P.S.106"R".

C18
4.14130
00m (4)

All minutes to be numbered in consecutive order.

THE BOY SCOUTS ASSOCIATION
FOUNDER: THE LORD BADEN-POWELL OF GILWELL.

COUNTY OF LONDON

Boy Scouts London Office,

> **NEW ADDRESS**
>
> **3, Cromwell Place**
> **S.W.7**
> Telephone: Kensington 1137/8

one: VICTORIA 6005

90.

he Commissioner of Police of the Metropolis,
ew Scotland Yard,
.W.1.

September 29th 1947.

ir,

Your ref. 14/47/53(A-2).

I have to thank you for your letter of the
5th September with reference to the Wedding of H.R.H.
he Princess Elizabeth on Thursday, 20th November, 1947.
am very hopeful that forty Rover Scouts will be
vailable to undertake messenger duties on this occasion,
nd will look forward to hearing further from you as to
he time and place of the parade and the officer to whom
he Rover Scouts should report.

I am, Sir,

Your obedient Servant,

JOHN WEEDEN,
London Secretary.

7 *Opposite:* The massive crowds at Trafalgar Square and the Strand as the procession returns to Buckingham Palace (MEPO 2/ 7967).

8 *Above:* One of the royal coaches leaves Buckingham Palace (MEPO 2/ 7967).

9 *Left:* The Duke and Duchess of Edinburgh acknowledge the cheers of the crowd.

10 *Right:* The British Embassy in Japan had to work hard to deflect the potential embarrassment of an official message of congratulations from a country still officially in a 'state of war' with Great Britain (FO 372/ 6090).

11 *Below:* The happy couple received telegrams of congratulations from across the world, including one from Juan Peron, President of Argentina (FO 372 /6090).

P.A.23/19/47.

United Kingdom Liaiso in Japan, British Embass Tokyo.

CONFIDENTIAL.   24th November, 19

T25921

12 DEC 1947

Dear Department,

With reference to my telegram No. the 20 November regarding certain messages congratulation and good wishes which were s me informally for The King and Princess Eli by Their Royal Highnesses Princes Chichibu Takamatsu of Japan, I enclose copies of the letters which were addressed to me on this

2.   As the messages from these two Pr their wives were sent to me privately and w risk of publicity, they were in a different from that which was to have been brought ro by an "Imperial Messenger" from the Emperor message of congratulation was also to have the Japanese Prime Minister.   These two me to have been published in the local press, that this would not be appropriate, given t war which legally exists between the two co I should perhaps explain that the approach to me by the staffs of the Emperor and the Minister through the American Diplomatic Se SCAP, which is the correct official channel to the existing American regulations. When colleague told me this, I asked him to do b tactfully to dissuade the Japanese Imperial authorities and the Prime Minister from pre matter, and Sebald was soon in a position t that he had been completely successful in d

3.   I should be grateful if you would know whether you consider that I acted righ avoiding the acceptance of the messages from and the Prime Minister, or whether in the i our future relations with Japan, I should ha the matter to take its course.

Yours ever,

epartment,
reign Office,
London, S.W.1.

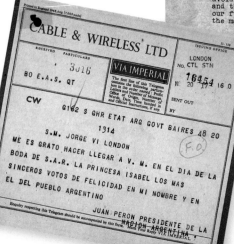

CABLE & WIRELESS LTD

VIA IMPERIAL

RECEIVED   PARTICULARS

ISSUING OFFICE

LONDON
No. CTL STN

N⁰ 20 17 16 0

16454 16 0

The first line of this Telegram contains the following particulars in the order named : Prefix, Letters and Number of Message, Office of Origin, Number of Words, Date, Time Handed in and Official Instructions, if any

3₀16

BO E.A.S. QT

CW

SENT OUT

BY

Q162 S GHR ETAT ARG GOVT BAIRES 48 20
1314
S.M. JORGE VI LONDON
ME ES GRATO HACER LLEGAR A V. M. EN EL DIA DE LA
BODA DE S.A.R. LA PRINCESA ISABEL LOS MAS
SINCEROS VOTOS DE FELICIDAD EN MI NOMBRE Y EN
EL DEL PUEBLO ARGENTINO

JUAN PERON PRESIDENTE DE LA
NACION ARGENTINA

(F.O.)

Enquiry respecting this Telegram should be accompanied by this form.   Mark Your Reply VIA IMPERIAL

With reference to your recent interview with an officer of this Department, I am directed by the Secretary of State to say that no objection will be raised to the production of a Union Flag defaced with representations of Her Royal Highness The Princess Elizabeth and Lieutenant Philip Mountbatten.

[HO 144/23364]

Traffic arrangements

Meetings in September began to record the detailed arrangements being made by the police for the processions and for getting all the guests, royal or not, into and out of the abbey [MEPO 2/7967]. Would the carriages make a sharp turn into Whitehall from the Mall, or sweep around the traffic island at the top of Whitehall? Detailed decisions had to be made, and graffiti in the margin of the minutes of these meetings illustrate the alternatives (plate 23).

Pages and pages of arrangements list the routes that cars carrying 'foreign royal personages and other distinguished guests who are attending Buckingham Palace to join the royal procession' would need to take. Royal guests not staying at Buckingham Palace were to be accommodated in several London hotels, including the Goring, the Dorchester, the Grosvenor Victoria, the Hyde Park and Claridge's, as well as various embassies and private addresses, so their journeys between where they were staying and the palace or the abbey had to be foolproof. Similarly, four of the bridesmaids had to be picked up from their homes in London, and a car had to be arranged for two princesses who were not going to the abbey but would have to be collected from their home and driven to Buckingham Palace for the wedding breakfast. And Lieutenant Mountbatten and his groomsman, the Marquess of Milford Haven, who were due to spend the night before the wedding at Kensington Palace, would need to be picked up there at 11am by one of the royal cars and driven to the Poets' Corner entrance to the abbey, with a police escort, to arrive there at 11.15am.

The documents record the impressive logistics worked out by the officials for transport between palace and abbey and back again for the main players. Dean's Yard was commandeered as a parking lot for carriages, cars and vans, and those who usually left their cars there were instructed to remove them before the day and park elsewhere, though they would be allowed back at 2pm. Residents and occupiers of Dean's Yard would have access on 20 November only by ticket.

The bride and her father were due to arrive at Westminster Abbey in the Irish State Coach, but she would return to the palace with her bridegroom in the Glass Coach. The last to arrive and the first to leave, the princess's coaches therefore had to be parked judiciously in Dean's Yard so that no traffic snarl-ups would ensue. It was all efficiently arranged, and a memo set out the order of parking, including transport for Palace officials and attendants such as valets and dressers [MEPO 2/7967]. Arrangements for these particular attendants were precise: they would leave Buckingham Palace 'at about 11.15am, AFTER Her Majesty the Queen's procession and BEFORE His Majesty the King's... and would proceed by the processional route to the West Door of the abbey'.

As well as these arrangements, other guests needed to know where they could park their cars and what the provisions were for them to be set down at the abbey and picked up again (page 34). R. Auriol Barker wrote: 'I feel that only a small proportion of the guests are likely, these days, to have chauffeur-driven cars, and that most would prefer to drive themselves and to walk between their cars and the abbey.' However, detailed instructions would have to be issued, along with tickets for windscreens and maps and routes for drivers and chauffeurs, and parking places allocated in many of the streets around Westminster.

Apart from access for those working in the abbey at the last minute, roads were to be closed off at 8am on the morning of 20 November. As a final precaution, airspace was secured:

the Minister of Civil Aviation has made regulations prohibiting flying within three miles of Trafalgar Square between 8am and 9pm on the day. [MEPO 2/7967]

A label for cars carrying wedding guests.

Flag: a souvenir of the wedding.

The police in force

Extra police were to be drafted in from all over London for the day, and arrangements made to divide them into the various sectors and allocate duties. They also had to be fed and watered – an additional problem with all the shortages – and then got home again to their stations at the end of the day. The Victory Parade provided a precedent on the question of extra rations for the police. Concessions on that occasion had allowed for three-fourteenths of an ounce of bacon for all meals served, plus four times that amount of belly bacon. The police caterers wanted the same this time, although in a telling comment on the even harsher state of the economy two years on, they acknowledged that

> the very critical bacon position may preclude the possibility
> of us getting any extra supplies of this commodity. In this
> event, a similar allowance of meat which could be pre-cooked
> in our kitchens would be just as useful as a solution to the
> sandwich problem, while an extra allowance of cheese would
> also be a great help. [MEPO 2/7967]

The alternative would be to serve 'sandwiches consisting almost exclusively of tinned meat and fish pastes, which would be not nearly substantial enough for men on duty for long hours under winter conditions.' A very welcome concession must have been the special licence granted to the police canteens to serve beer outside normal hours between 3pm and 5.30pm.

The departure on honeymoon of the bride and groom was another factor that the police had to take into account – rather rapidly, as it was not until 13 November that they were informed of the arrangements for this part of the day. A letter from the Assistant Commissioner of the Metropolitan Police to one of his counterparts makes the urgency clear:

> We have just heard that the bride and bridegroom will be going away from Waterloo on the afternoon of the 20th. May we keep your policemen on for this? It should be possible to dismiss them anyhow by 4.30pm. If you agree we shall be most grateful. [MEPO 2/7967]

Having their cakes...

Official cake
Made with ingredients from the Australian Girl Guides, baked by McVitie & Price.
Features: 900lb weight; 9ft high; gothic design.

One of several other cakes
Made by Huntley & Palmers.
Features: six sides; four tiers, some with images of royal family.

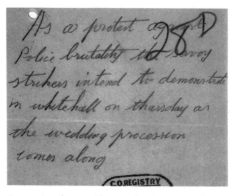

As a protest against
Police brutality the Savoy
strikers intend to demonstrate
in whitehall on thursday as
the wedding procession
comes along

C.O.REGISTRY

A warning from strikers at the Savoy Hotel.

Details, details…

For Barker and other officials of the Ministry of Works, no detail was too unimportant to be overlooked. The most suitable chairs for the royal guests were usually housed in the State Rooms of St James's Palace – could they be borrowed and what arrangements would need to be made to transport them to the abbey and return them afterwards? Barker sorted it out. The large numbers of extra servants who would be in attendance on royal guests at Buckingham Palace would put a strain on the provision of blankets there – could Mr Barker loan the palace 100 extra blankets? Yes, he could. What if the day turned out to be foggy? Fog lamps were gathered together in readiness, and the normal street lighting would be turned on if necessary. What arrangements were to be made for the sale of official programmes on the day? The Boy Scouts were recruited and were to be stationed in Green Park and St James's Park to sell them; the revenue would go to King George's Jubilee Trust.

It was not just along the processional routes that details

had to be meticulously worked out. Access to St James's Park would be restricted on the day of the wedding, so how were the milkman and baker to deliver to the park café that day? The answer was to give them letters allowing them access 'on duty', but the café was also advised to get in supplies early on the night before. How about flying flags on government buildings? On the occasions of several previous royal marriages flags had been flown, so Barker assumed that 'it will be His Majesty's pleasure that flags should similarly be flown on 20 November'.

He meticulously recorded the costs incurred by the Ministry: awning West Door £115, carpets £83, draping in chapel £9, curtain at abbey door £15, Chapter House floor covering £10, loan of 800 chairs £50, other awnings £300, Whitehall decorations £400, banners by Buckingham Palace £544. Plus their share of the stand in the abbey; altogether a total of something over £1,500.

As 20 November approached, all these arrangements began to come together. Seating plans in the abbey had been agreed, with the immediate royal family in the chancel and other royal guests, cabinet ministers and dignitaries allotted seats in the choir stalls; indeed, there were so many foreign royals coming to London for the wedding that some of the government and diplomatic grandees had to ballot for these privileged positions. All the other guests were placed on the lengthy seating plans, and tickets issued for the restricted vantage points outside the abbey.

The wedding's effect on normal business had also to be factored in. The processional route was due to be sanded on the day to make it smoother for jolting carriages, a task that would be carried out by the City of Westminster's Engineering and Surveying Department; they were also asked whether they would sand the route on Sunday 16 November when a full rehearsal was due to take place. They agreed, but added that they would also need to carry out road repairs in Whitehall and Parliament Street that weekend, since it would be impossible to do so on the previous weekend because of the Remembrance ceremony at the Cenotaph. However, they 'would make every effort to carry out the repairs without interference with the rehearsal'. For the officials working indefatigably behind the scenes, it was all nearly ready.

The wedding presents

Over 2,500 wedding presents were flooding in from all over the world, ranging from the spectacular to the mundane. Very welcome practical gifts in those days of austerity included clothing and the food items already described. The princess and her husband-to-be were also presented with items for the home such as a sewing machine, a Hoover vacuum cleaner, an automatic potato peeler, a refrigerator, an Anglepoise lamp and a bath sponge. They received many dinner services too, several of them still in use today, including a Sèvres service presented by the government and people of France, a Chinese porcelain service given by President and Madame Chiang Kai-Shek of the Chinese Republic and a Royal Worcester service from the Brigade of Guards. A very personal item was a piece of lace, intended as a tray cover, woven with his own hands by Mahatma Gandhi; Queen Mary was reportedly disgusted by this object because she thought it was a loincloth.

The various armed services had raised subscriptions for presents, and now gave the couple gifts bought with some of the money and cheques for the rest, either to be spent as they chose or given to charity. The Shah of Iran sent a carpet, which somehow missed the flight it was supposed to be on and had to be delivered later. And some of the presents caused behind-the-scenes anxieties. Would it be acceptable, for instance, for the recent enemy, Italy, to send something? Yes it would, and the princess would be very grateful

Radio and television

The BBC had been closed down on 1 September 1939, half-way through a Mickey Mouse cartoon. It did not broadcast again until June 1946, when it started again with the same cartoon.

New radio shows in 1947 included:

· *Much Binding in the Marsh*
· *How Does Your Garden Grow*, later renamed *Gardeners' Question Time* and still running
· *Twenty Questions*
· *Round Britain Quiz*, still running

1947 also saw the first television broadcast of the *Last Night of the Proms*.

for some lengths of silk, the design to be left to the good taste of the Italians. What about a gift from the Republic of Indonesia? No, because 'the government has been recognized *de facto* and not *de jure* so if HRH were to accept a gift in the name of the Republic it might perhaps be interpreted, however unwarrantably, as implying recognition of a fuller character'; a gift from the people of Indonesia would, however, be perfectly acceptable. How about brocade from the President of Syria and his wife? Yes, but an embassy official wrote, 'although all Damascus brocade is beautiful, some of it is less suited to British tastes, so I have arranged for my wife to see what is being proposed.' The eventual decision was to send a roll of white silk brocade with an ancient Persian design and gold thread running through it.

Perhaps most spectacular were the presents which the bride received from her own family. These were mostly

A rejected design for a commemorative brooch.

splendid pieces of jewellery, among them several pieces from Queen Mary that she had been given on the occasion of her own wedding, including a splendid diamond stomacher and bracelets, as well as a Boucheron ruby and diamond necklace. The king and queen gave their daughter a sapphire and diamond necklace and earring suite that had been made in the mid-19th century by Garrard, a pair of diamond chandelier earrings and the two beautiful strings of pearls that she was to wear on her wedding day. On 18 November, the Princess went to view the presents with her parents at a party at St James's Palace where they were on display.

The first celebrations

The king and queen held another party on 18 November at Buckingham Palace for more than 1,000 people. Among them were many guests from around the world who were in London for the wedding, as well as the Prime Minister, Clement Attlee, members of his cabinet and Winston Churchill. On the following day, 19 November, the final wedding rehearsal was held at the abbey, and that night Buckingham Palace was floodlit, proving to be 'a brave sight, with the brightness of the spectacle enhanced by the individual lighting of the semicircle of banners bearing the initials

Wedding gifts

Among the 2,500 presents were:

Pope Pius XII: pair of Meissen chocolate pots.

The people of Kenya: Sagana hunting lodge.

The Aga Khan: a thoroughbred filly.

The Mayor and City of London: a diamond fringe necklace.

The RAF and WAAF: a grand piano.

The princess's friends: a pair of silver gilt candelabra and a Rockingham dinner service.

The Nizam of Hyderabad: a diamond foliate necklace.

The Army: an 18th-century mahogany sideboard.

President Truman: an engraved Steuben vase.

E and P'. London was a party scene, as crowds of spectators descended on the capital to sightsee and enjoy themselves before claiming their places along the processional routes for the following day. They gathered in their thousands outside the floodlit palace, and were rewarded by appearances on the balcony of the engaged couple alongside the king, the queen and Princess Margaret.

The capital city was coming alive. Whitehall was a centre of great activity, as the new flowers were planted in the window boxes of government buildings. The awnings outside Westminster Abbey were receiving their final touches of red and gold decoration. Shop windows in the West End were festooned with flags and bunting, as well as large photos of the princess and the bridegroom. As day turned to evening the streets began to take on a carnival air. People were out in their thousands, and vendors of roast chestnuts and official programmes were doing a roaring trade. People had come to London from all over the country and the world, and many of those who had driven in from outside the city had clearly hoarded scarce petrol so that they could be there in the capital for this great occasion.

By the middle of the evening the best places along the route and in front of both palace and abbey had been claimed, with spectators well prepared for the night chill. As *The Times* reported: 'Women were in the majority, and they brought with them a variety of comforts, ranging from Balaclava helmets to groundsheets. "It will be well worth it," said one.'

The Ball Supper Room at Buckingham Palace was being made ready for the wedding breakfast, and Mr Edward Goodyear was arranging the floral decorations of pink carnations, white heather and mimosa, much of it sent as a gift from the south of France. The cakes were placed there too, and the princess came to view them and spent some time in the room talking to the representatives of their makers. Later that evening, after her fiancé had left for his stag night with his uncle and his naval friends, she responded to the throngs outside shouting 'We want Elizabeth' and singing 'All the nice girls love a sailor' by appearing alone on the floodlit palace balcony, waving and blowing kisses to the crowds.

And it was on that day too, 19 November, that Lieutenant

Home, Sweet Home

The royal couple were looking for a suitable London residence while Clarence House was being refurbished. Horace Kadoorie, British citizen and wealthy Shanghai businessman, offered them the use of his London house at 6 Princes Gate: 'The Ethiopian Legation is, at present, in residence there, and I should have to give them due warning should Her Royal Highness graciously accept.' The Foreign Office advised, 'I hardly think we need do anything.'

Mountbatten ceased to be a mere commoner, but was invested by his future father-in-law with a number of honours. The front page of *The Times* of 20 November was, as usual, a full page of small ads. But to the right of the masthead it carried the announcement 'Royal Dukedom for Bridegroom', and inside was the formal report of Philip's new status:

> Buckingham Palace announced last night: The king today conferred the honour of knighthood on Lieutenant Philip Mountbatten RN and invested him with the insignia of a Knight Companion of the Most Noble Order of the Garter. His Majesty has been pleased to authorize the use of the prefix His Royal Highness by Lieutenant Philip Mountbatten RN and to approve that the dignity of a Dukedom of the United Kingdom be conferred upon him by the name, style and title of Baron Greenwich of Greenwich in the County of London, Earl of Merioneth and Duke of Edinburgh.

Princess Elizabeth had been made a Lady of the Garter a few days previously, which made her senior in the order to her fiancé. And although he was now HRH and a duke, Philip was not at this time created a prince of the United Kingdom; that honour was to be conferred on him ten years later by his wife, who by then was queen.

3

THE WEDDING DAY

So it was as HRH The Duke of Edinburgh that the bridegroom made his way to Westminster Abbey, with his groomsman, cousin and close friend the Marquess of Milford Haven, on the morning of 20 November. The two of them had spent the previous evening at the Dorchester Hotel, along with Lord Mountbatten and several naval friends, celebrating Philip's stag night. The *Daily Mirror* carried a photo of the occasion the following day, showing Philip, his uncle and his friends looking happy and relaxed. It reported that they had eaten lemon sole, pheasant and fruit salad with ice cream, and had drunk champagne with the meal and coffee and beer afterwards.

The article also carried the light-hearted information that, after the photographer had taken his shots of the party, Mountbatten suggested that the camera be handed over so that he in turn could take photos of the press. What the reporter did not go on to say was that, after he had duly taken the photographs, Mountbatten had removed the flash bulbs from the camera and smashed them so that there could be no further pictures. The gentlemen of the press appeared to take this in good heart – these were more polite and deferential times, and the word paparazzo, along with all its later connotations of intrusiveness, had yet to be coined.

After their convivial evening, Philip and David Milford Haven returned to Kensington Palace where, as a valet was later to write, their rooms were simple and unglamorous. Philip was up early the next morning – his valet brought him tea at 7am – to get ready for the momentous day. Both groom and best man wore naval uniform, Philip's adorned with his newly acquired Garter star and the Greek Order of the Redeemer, to which he had been appointed by his cousin, King George II of Greece. The royal car duly arrived to take them to the abbey where, as press and broadcasters noted, he and Milford Haven were like any other young bridegroom and best man awaiting the arrival of the bride: sitting chatting in their places at the foot of the altar, toying with their ceremonial swords and occasionally, somewhat nervously, glancing back towards the door of the abbey, through which the royal family and eventually the princess herself would walk.

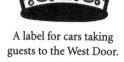

A label for cars taking guests to the West Door.

Meanwhile at Buckingham Palace, Princess Elizabeth too was up early and was also brought a morning cup of tea by her loyal maid Bobo while it was still dark. In her later book about her time with the royal family, *The Little Princesses*, their governess Marion Crawford, always known as 'Crawfie', described going to Elizabeth's room and finding her, still in her dressing gown, excitedly peeping out of the window at the crowds outside in the freezing dawn.

Her portrayal of Princess Elizabeth on her wedding morning certainly has the ring of truth. She was no doubt like any other young bride on her wedding day – excited, nervous, slightly overwhelmed. And although Elizabeth was undoubtedly more used than most brides to glamorous frocks and jewellery, she too must have felt exhilarated at the thought of the glorious outfit she was about to don. Norman Hartnell, who had designed the wedding dress, had delivered it to the palace the night before; now, at 9am, he arrived with his entourage to help the bride into it. He had worked in complete secrecy for three months on both bride's and bridesmaids' dresses, even whitewashing the windows of his Bruton Street workroom so that no curious eyes or lenses could spy on him. His manager had travelled widely to obtain the materials for the dresses, including the 10,000 seed pearls for the bridal gown that had come from America. Hartnell had also had to counter worries that the silk he was using had been produced by 'enemy' silkworms in Japan or Italy; but he was able to assert firmly that the silkworms were in fact from China.

The dress was both simple in line and spectacular in decoration. In ivory silk with long sleeves and a round, slightly scalloped neckline, it fitted tightly to the waist and then fell in wide, gentle folds to the feet. The motifs embroidered on it were inspired by Botticelli's painting *Primavera* – a symbol of hope and rebirth after the horrors and deprivation of the war years and their aftermath. The pearls were arranged as the white roses of York, intertwined with ears of corn picked out in crystals. Finely fitted to Elizabeth's slim figure, the dress looked stunning (plate 13).

The beautiful, 15-ft-long train that fell from the shoulders was equally splendid (plate 14). It was embroidered with a multitude of stars interspersed with leaves and ears of corn; 350 girls had worked on it for seven weeks in Braintree, Essex, under the supervision of Hartnell's head embroiderer, Miss Flora Ballard. Its heaviness, however, was to prove a problem for the two young page boys: as the *Daily Mirror* of 21 November reported,

> As they move towards the altar after the vows, the train, carried by the boy pages, Prince William of Gloucester and Prince Michael of Kent, catches on the steps. Philip looks over his shoulder before he walks forward, and again when the princess pauses. But the king on her left and the best man on her right stoop to free the train, and the pair, married now, walk along to the altar.

The princess wore her long, light veil thrown back from her face, in the custom of royal brides always, which revealed the sparkle of her pearl and diamond earrings. Once the property of one of George III's daughters, they were a gift to the princess on her 20th birthday from her grandmother, Queen Mary. The veil was held in place by 'something borrowed' – her mother's diamond fringe tiara, which incorporated diamonds that had been given as a wedding present to Queen Mary by Queen Victoria.

The tiara was to cause the first alarm of the morning when it snapped while being put in place on her head. It was hastily repaired – and it was then that another dreadful realization dawned. The pearls that the princess wished to wear, a wedding present from her parents, were locked away with all the other presents at St James's Palace. Somehow no one had thought to remove them from the display. Elizabeth's new private secretary, Jock Colville, was hastily summoned and asked to make a frenzied dash to retrieve the pearls through all the thronging onlookers.

Broadcasting the royal wedding

Inside Westminster Abbey, the BBC was provided with sound-proof booths in the triforium, from where Wynford Vaughan-Thomas described the ceremony to an audience of millions round the world.

Outside, film and television cameras, and radio microphones, were in place all along the processional route, with Richard Dimbleby, John Snagg, Frank Gillard, Peter Scott and Audrey Russell positioned to record the events. Film cameras were allowed inside Buckingham Palace to record the joyful return of the royal family.

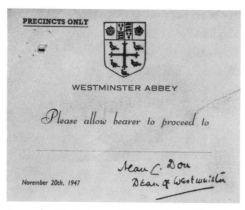

PRECINCTS ONLY

WESTMINSTER ABBEY

Please allow bearer to proceed to

_____

November 20th, 1947

Jean C. Don
Dean of Westminster

A pass for Westminster Abbey on the wedding day.

As he later recounted, he ran down to the forecourt where a car was just drawing up and leapt into it – only to find King Haakon of Norway getting out. 'By all means use my car, young man,' the king said; 'but do let me get out of it first.' The car raced to St James's Palace, but the detectives guarding the presents there refused to accept that Colville was who he said he was. It was only after frantic pleading – and after an abortive telephone call to Buckingham Palace which failed to connect – that they eventually allowed him to take the pearls. He arrived back at the palace, firmly clutching them in his pocket, with just minutes to spare.

There was yet another alarm that morning when the bridal bouquet was mislaid. The unfortunate footman who had taken charge of it when it was delivered to the palace that morning remembered bringing it upstairs, but could not now think what he had done with it. Relief descended when he suddenly – mercifully – recalled that he had placed it in a cool cupboard to keep it fresh.

It took Norman Hartnell over an hour to array the bride in her beautiful outfit. He also had the eight bridesmaids to dress. There was the usual bustle and excitement as everyone got ready. And soon, in exact accord with the schedules, the various entourages were ready to leave Buckingham Palace and make their way along the processional route to Westminster Abbey.

Behind the scenes

It had been a cold, wet November night, but the grey morning light saw the rain stopping and the crowds, who had filled every vantage point and cheerfully braved the elements, radiated undimmed enthusiasm and happiness. The policemen and servicemen – bussed in from all over London and the south-east – mustered at 7am to take up their stations. The pressure of the crowds was so great that the workmen due to put the crush barriers in place could not carry out the work, and the policemen had to step in to help. Police along

Abbey officials

The Dean of Westminster Abbey, Alan Don, met the princess at the West Door and preceded her up the nave. The ceremony was performed by the Archbishop of Canterbury, Geoffrey Fisher, supported by the Archbishop of York, Cyril Garbett, who delivered the address to the newly married couple.

the route also had to deal with members of other organizations, such as the St John's Ambulance Brigade and the Boy Scouts, who – in their semi-official capacity – tried to claim privileged positions in front of the barriers as the time for the processions drew near. One particularly aggrieved memo suggested that in future 'a well-established police line should not be cluttered up' by such people; he had had to deal with 'large numbers of the tallest brand of Boy Scouts who had been told by their officers to accommodate themselves in the police line. I chased some of them away to take their chance with the general public.' The police also had problems at the bottom of Victoria Street with numbers of chauffeurs who, having dropped guests at the abbey and parked in their designated places, congregated there to get a view of the arrivals at the abbey's West Door.

Police were also in place wherever members of the public

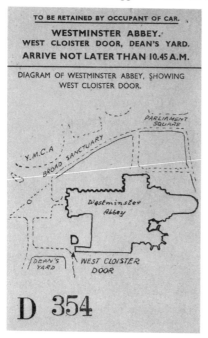

A permit to drive to Westminster Abbey.

might scale walls or climb on monuments to get a better view. The bomb-damaged building in Carlton Gardens was particularly vulnerable, as was the subway entrance outside Malaya House in Trafalgar Square, where the glass panels might be broken by people climbing on them. The only place where climbing could not be prevented was the Royal Artillery Boer War Memorial on the Mall. The two police constables stationed there worked hard, but could not keep climbers off.

Others that morning were handling the complex traffic arrangements. The key roads were closed at 8am, but cars and other forms of transport picking up royal guests, brides-maids and Lieutenant Mountbatten and his groomsman were being threaded through the crowds on prearranged and closely defined routes. A police memo recorded the arrangements that had been put in place to ensure that the bridegroom's car 'moves exactly to schedule ... from the Royal Mews to Kensington Palace and from there to the processional route at Queen's Gardens'. The Archbishop of Canterbury's car was to leave Lambeth Palace at 10.30am carrying the archbishop and his wife. It was due to set Mrs Fisher down at the West Door at 10.40am and to take Dr Fisher round to the West Cloister Door. Yet again, on another level, the coach that had left Sandringham at 5.15am to bring members of the royal household staff to London had to be routed so that it could set some of them down at the abbey and others at the tradesmen's entrance at Buckingham Palace.

A brief pencilled note in the police files reveals that they dealt with 2,502 casualties from the thousands of onlookers (page 102). Given the huge crowds, this seems like a satisfactory result. It is clear that police and officials had all conducted themselves with efficiency and good humour on what was a long and no doubt stressful day.

The wedding guests

Almost as soon as the engagement was announced, the Foreign Office had to deal with numbers of other diplomatic enquiries as to who would, and who would not, be invited. With the country so recently in the grip of a devastating war and still under the lash of economic privations, over-extravagance in the form of thousands of invitations could not be contemplated. There would still be 2,600 guests invited to the service in the abbey; but it was decided early on that requests for invitations from foreign dignitaries would be met with a polite refusal on the grounds that the wedding was predominantly a family and domestic affair (plate 3).

The guest list was therefore a mixture of holders of high government and diplomatic office in Great Britain, as well as members of the extended European royal family along with their suites, and courtiers and friends. The Prime Minister,

MEMORANDUM.

ROYAL WEDDING - 20TH NOVEMBER, 1947.

Information has been received that a small van will leave Moyes Stevens, Florists, with bouquets, etc., to arrive at the Great West Door at about 10.30 a.m.

An "Emergency Services" label has been issued and the car will arrive by way of Victoria Street, to leave by way of Tothill Street, etc.

(Sgd) S. Wells.

Superintendent.

12 *Above:* Nothing was left to chance in the meticulous plans. This memorandum was issued to ensure that the florist's van got to Westminster Abbey on schedule (MEPO 2/ 7967).

13 *Right:* Princess Elizabeth arrives for the ceremony in her Norman Hartnell wedding gown. The BBC commentator Peter Scott described the happy scene: 'This is our princess … going to marry the man she loves.'

WHITEHALL,
LONDON, S.W.1.

24th November, 1947.

My dear Commissioner;

I have received from Her Royal Highness The Princess Elizabeth and His Royal Highness The Duke of Edinburgh a telegram in the following words.—

"Right Hon. Chuter Ede, Home Secretary, Whitehall, S.W.1.

Please convey to the members of the Police Force and Special Constabulary in London our sincere thanks for their messages of congratulations and our deep appreciation of all they did to make our Wedding Day such a happy one – Elizabeth and Philip."

Yours sincerely,

J. Chuter Ede

Sir Harold Scott, K.C.B., K.B.E.

16 *Left:* In the midst of all the excitement of their wedding, Elizabeth and Philip expressed many thanks to those whose hard work had contributed to the day. Here the Home Secretary passes on the bride and groom's appreciation to the Metropolitan Police Commissioner (MEPO 2/ 7967).

14 *Opposite:* The royal couple receive the blessing from the Archbishop of Canterbury. King George VI is on the bride's left and Philip's best man, the Marquess of Milford Haven, is on the bridegroom's right.

15 *Right:* Details of the bride's procession from Westminster Abbey's West Door (MEPO 2/7967). 'Supported by Her Father, The King', the bride followed palace and abbey officials, choir and clergy.

PROCESSION OF THE BRIDE.

Comptroller, Lord Chamberlain's Office,
Lieut.-Colonel Sir Terence Nugent.

Master of the Household,
Lieut.-Colonel Hon. Sir Piers Legh

The King's Scholars.

The Choir.

The Minor Canons.

The Canon's Verger.

The Canons.

The Right Hon. H. U. Willink
(High Bailiff of Westminster)

The Dean's Verger

The Earl of Halifax
(High Steward of Westminster)

The Dean of Westminster.

THE BRIDE,

Supported by Her Father,

THE KING,

attended by Her Royal Highness's Pages:

His Royal Highness Prince Michael of
Kent,

His Royal Highness Prince William of
Gloucester,

and followed by Her Royal Highness's Bridesmaids:

Her Royal Highness Princess Alexandra
of Kent

The Lady Mary Cambridge
The Honourable Pamela Mountbatten
Miss Diana Bowes-Lyon
Private Secretary to The Bride,
John Colville, Esq.

Her Royal Highness The Princess Margaret

The Lady Caroline Montagu-Douglas-Scott
The Lady Elizabeth Lambart
The Honourable Margaret Elphinstone
La'y-in-Waiting to The Bride,
The Lady Margaret Seymour

Suite of His Majesty The King:

Groom-in-Waiting,
Major Arthur Penn
Equerry-in-Waiting,
Lieutenant-Commander Peter Ashmore, R.N.

Lord-in-Waiting,
The Earl of Eldon
Equerry-in-Waiting,
Wing Commander Peter Townsend.

" . . . You will be interested to know that I was in the Abbey for the service. I had been given a pass to the precincts – but not a place in the Abbey. However, just as the King and the Princess arrived I was passing a small door which (if you know the Abbey well, you'll remember) leads through the Chapel of St. George. It was open and no one was standing there to say me nay. I just quietly walked through the door, through the Chapel and as still no one was there to say I mustn't, I was then just at the West Door of the Abbey. I stood there the whole time hardly believing it was true that I was there, but more appreciative of my good fortune than I can express and more impressed by the beauty of what I witnessed than I've ever been in my life before. I can't imagine that in the future I'll ever see anything as lovely. When the Princess and her husband came down the Nave they were a radiant couple. I could have touched them as they passed."

17 *Above:* Mrs Wilcox, a tourist in London, records her amazing luck in making it into the Abbey on the day (MEPO 2/7967). The letter was sent to the police by her friend, and prompted a hasty inquiry.

18 *Right:* The newly married couple progress proudly down the aisle followed by the page boys, Princess Margaret and the other bridesmaids. The bells of Westminster Abbey rang out as the doors opened to reveal the cheering crowds outside.

19 *Right:* A polite but firm request from the police catering service for an extension of licensing hours (MEPO 2/ 7967). Supplies of beer helped to keep up morale on the long day.

20 *Below:* A young boy is rescued from the press of the crowd and helped into a policeman's arms (MEPO 2/ 7960).

METROPOLITAN POLICE FOOD SERVICE

TELEPHONE:
HOP 3045

222/4 Borough High Street,
S.E.1.

AKY/KED.

4th November 1947

A.C. 'A',
New Scotland Yard.

Royal Wedding

May permission please be given for the Special Canteens established in connection with the above to sell intoxicating liquor (i.e. beer) from 10 a.m. onwards on the day.

This authority was given for the Canteens on the Mechanised Route for the Victory Celebrations, although the other Canteens in the West End were only allowed to function for normal licensing hours. This led to a certain amount of complaint, and I feel that 10 a.m. onwards would be very desirable on this occasion.

Canteens ... ld be those
.../47/53(A-2)
he exception
ch are not allowed

R.

BUCKINGHAM PALACE

22nd November, 1947.

Sir,

Before Princess Elizabeth left for the Honeymoon Her Royal Highness asked me to thank on her behalf whoever was responsible for the erection of the banners in front of Buckingham Palace, for the fluorescent lighting which illuminated them so charmingly after dark, and for the flood lighting of the Palace. The Princess felt that it was particularly pleasing that it should have been found possible, in these difficult times, to add a few touches of light and gaiety to the scene and that the results contributed to the success of the occasion.

Yours truly,

John Colville

Private Secretary to
The Princess Elizabeth.

21 *Above:* The royal party greet joyful crowds from the balcony of Buckingham Palace. From left to right: King George VI, Princess Margaret, Lady Mary Cambridge, the bride and bridegroom, Queen Elizabeth, Queen Mary.

22 *Left:* The princess conveyed her thanks to the Minister of Works for the floodlit display, part of the day's magic (WORK 21/ 254).

23 *Right:* Details of the wedding route were planned by officials back in September (MEPO 2/ 7967). The marginalia here depict the possibilities that were discussed.

24 *Below:* The new Duke and Duchess of Edinburgh return from the Abbey in the famous Glass Coach.

NOTES FOR CONFERENCE

3B

1. Is Queen's Gardens to be kept clear on all sides   Yes

2. On the Return Journey will T.M. the King and Queen enter the Palace by way of Queen's Gardens NORTH side or SOUTH side

3. On the return journey will the Bride and Bridegroom turn sharp right from Constitution Hill to enter the Palace, or will they circle the Q.V.Memorial.

4. When turning into Constitution Hill from Piccadilly, will the Royal Carriage use Queen's Road (between the Wellington and Artillery Memorials) or will it continue past the Artillery Memorial Island and turn between that island and the Machine Gun Memorial Island

5. When turning from The Mall into Whitehall, will the processions make sharp turns into Whitehall or make wide sweeps round the island in the centre of Whitehall.   Yes

6. Nearside of all refuges

7. Fog and inclement weather - alternative arrgts.

MILITARY

1. Military lining route from B.Palace to Westminster Abbey or to S.W. Corner of Parliament square. No troops in Broad Sanctuary

2. Thicken at [...] orough Yard; [...] Cenotaph

25 *Above:* The happy couple on honeymoon at Broadlands, Hampshire.
26 *Below:* A telegram of thanks (MEPO 2 /7967).

Clement Attlee, was there, as were Winston Churchill, the Leader of the Opposition, selected members of the cabinet and the shadow cabinet and other senior Members of Parliament. Ambassadors to the Court of St James from foreign countries were also invited, along with members of foreign royal families who were relations or friends of the British royal family. Invitations to the latter were at the specific request of the king and queen.

Some foreign dignitaries tried very hard to obtain an invitation. The Portuguese Duke of Palmella, for example, informed the Foreign Office that he was urging his government to despatch a fine wedding present to Princess Elizabeth and emphasized that it would be 'from England's Oldest Ally'. The Vatican also hoped for an invitation, and the Prince of Monaco was very anxious for his grandson, Prince Rainier, to attend; his representative made several approaches to the British Embassy in Paris and to the Foreign Office in London on the matter, and even wrote directly to Philip to ask for an invitation. Although it was clear that, within diplomatic

Music at the wedding

Before the service:
Elgar *Sonata in G Major*
Widor *Andante Cantabile*
Bach *Fugue Alla Giga*
Bach *Jesu, joy of man's desiring*
Handel *The Water Music* (selections)
Parry *Bridal March*

The service:
Lyte *Praise, my soul, the King of Heaven*
Bairstow *Psalm LXVII, God be merciful unto us*
McKie *We wait for thy loving kindness, O God*
Crimond *The Lord's my shepherd*
Gibbons *Amen*
Wesley *Blessed be the God and Father*
Mendelssohn *Wedding March*

circles, 'our relations with Monaco are a trifle strained due to the tendency in some quarters to deny the sovereignty of the Principality', the refusal of this request was in line with all such refusals, which were 'intended to rule out Presidents of Republics and Oriental monarchs (even if they do send wedding presents)'.

Processions to the abbey

Most of the guests went straight to Westminster Abbey. Those taking part in the processions from Buckingham Palace to the abbey and back again were the most important royals and aristocrats from home and abroad, along with the royal equerries, ladies-in-waiting and other attendants. The police files list some 30 cars which processed along the Mall and down Whitehall from the palace at the start of

proceedings, carrying the bridegroom's mother, Princess Andrew of Greece, in the first car, followed by the other dignitaries. Next came the cars carrying Queen Mary and her suite, which included the Dowager Duchess of Devonshire and the Dowager Countess of Airlie, who had earlier been picked up from their homes and taken to Marlborough House so that they could accompany the queen.

The Royal Coat of Arms used on official letters.

Now came the carriage processions, set out

Princess Margaret

Princess Margaret, born on 21 August 1930, was 17 at the time of Elizabeth's wedding. As her rank required, she was chief bridesmaid, and she accompanied the bridal party into St Edward's Chapel for the signing of the register. At the palace, she appeared on the balcony with the royal family, and in the official photographs stood on the groom's immediate left.

in all their formal military detail by Major-General J.C.O. Marriott, in a London District, Special District Order. The troops lining the route were to be 'at four paces interval measured from heel to heel, and one pace from the kerb'.

The carriage processions left precisely on time and waiting for them, among the thousands of spectators, was the world's press. In Westminster Abbey, the BBC presenter Wynford Vaughan-Thomas was in the booth in the triforium getting ready for the innovative radio broadcast of a royal wedding, and in the streets outside his BBC colleagues – Richard Dimbleby, Peter Scott, John Snagg, Audrey Russell and Frank Gillard – were at their posts. Also in London for the occasion were more than 1,600 reporters, photographers, radio and film commentators and cameramen from all over the world, including China, India, Malaya, all the western European countries and even from the Soviet Union.

After the BBC coverage began with the sonorous announcement 'This is London', followed by the bells of Big Ben striking eleven times, Frank Gillard, standing at the foot of the Victoria Memorial outside Buckingham Palace, was the first to chronicle the events of the day. His slightly plummy voice can still be heard on the bakelite records held in the BBC and British Library Sound Archives, to the backdrop of the cheering crowds and the clip-clop of horses' hooves. The excitement was palpable, and indeed all the broadcasters that day frequently stopped their commentaries and turned their microphones on the crowds so that listeners could hear for themselves how happy and noisy the occasion was. For a short time it was clear that, on that cold, grey November morning, the people of Britain were willing to forget the shortages and the austerity with which they were surrounded and rejoice with the royal family in the happiness of the occasion.

Gillard's coverage started just a minute before the procession of Her Majesty the Queen was due to drive out of the inner forecourt of the palace; he reported the relief felt by the crowds that the rain had stopped and that the temperature had relented slightly, and then told his listeners that the mother of the bride was safely on her way to the abbey. He could now see 'the Sovereign's escort of the Lifeguards and the Blues on black and brown horses for the bride's procession', and a distant white figure being helped into the Irish State Coach, taking her place next to her father, the king, dressed in his uniform as Admiral of the Fleet. The excitement grew as the moment approached when the bride would leave the forecourt; as Gillard reported, 'The crowds on my right have broken through the police cordon – it's hopeless for the police to try to get them back.' But the National Anthem pealed out again, and orders were shouted in the background as the bride left the palace 'for the last time as a single woman from the home of her parents. Let the sounds speak for themselves.' Once again the sound of hooves and huge, swelling cheers. 'There she goes, a lovely figure… sitting to the right of the king. A sight to lift the heart as they vanish down there into the grey of this misty November day'.

The windows of the Irish State Coach and the Glass Coach had, as the *Daily Mirror* reported, been 'treated with an anti-dim substance so that they won't steam up and disappoint the crowds'. Moreover, both coaches were fitted with 3ft-long aluminium

Attendants of the bride and bridegroom

Best man: David, the Marquess of Milford Haven

Pages: Prince Michael of Kent and Prince William of Gloucester

Chief bridesmaid: The Princess Margaret

Bridesmaids:
Princess Alexandra of Kent
Lady Mary Cambridge
Lady Caroline Montagu-Douglas-Scott
The Hon Pamela Mountbatten
Lady Elizabeth Lambart
Miss Diana Bowes Lyon
The Hon Margaret Elphinstone

hot water bottles under the seats to keep their occupants warm. But the cold outside did nothing to dampen the cheering and waving of the spectators along the Mall as the bride passed by. Audrey Russell at Admiralty Arch now took up the commentary. Along with other journalists, she had been shown the material and the design for the dress and described it as something 'that came out of a fairy tale – a very modern one, but with a feeling of the past, an ethereal feel'. The princess looked 'dignified and serene' as the Irish State Coach, with its footmen in their scarlet livery, could be seen framed under Admiralty Arch before turning right into Whitehall. Again, the day's sounds reverberated: cheers and screams from the crowd, shouted commands and the clattering of horses' hooves echoing against the walls of the arch.

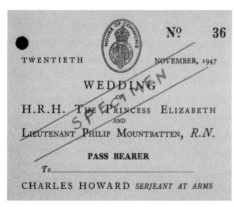

A pass to New Palace Yard, Westminster.

The service

On the following day, 21 November, *The Times* memorably described the scene in Westminster Abbey as the guests waited for the arrival of the bride. Under banner headlines 'Splendour of Ceremony' and 'A Family Event', 'Our Special Correspondent' stirringly wrote:

> Never more vividly than at yesterday's ceremony at Westminster Abbey can the spectator have felt the peculiar significance of the modern imperial monarchy as the mediating influence between the vast solemnity of the governance of nations and the human simplicities out of which nations are built up... This was a family event, transacted in the bosom of history.

He went on to talk of 'the mighty past to which this day a new and hopeful chapter was to be added' and drew attention to the royal tombs of 'all but one of the queens who have reigned in their own right in the two kingdoms' behind the abbey's altar.

Richard Dimbleby had been all morning at the West Door of the abbey, describing the arrival of the guests and then of the royal processions. There had been so many famous people pouring into the abbey that morning that he had difficulty identifying them. 'But now Her Majesty Queen Mary arrives in one of the old-fashioned cars she likes to use... a lovely, tall, regal figure, she walks slowly in, in her beautiful dress of aquamarine, to the strains of the National Anthem.' This was the first time since before the war that there had been such pageantry on display; for over six years the Household Cavalry had laid aside their full ceremonial dress and now, in front of all the spectators revelling in the unaccustomed colour and glitter, they looked shining and glorious in their metal breastplates and brightly coloured uniforms.

It was nearly time for the procession of the bride to reach the abbey. Outside, at his station by St Margaret's, the BBC commentator Peter Scott described 'the great wave of cheering, the pageantry, the colour, the majesty' as her coach with its escorts and outriders came into view. And then he caught the feeling: '…but this is something quite personal, too. This is our princess, and this great affectionate crowd is watching her going to marry the man she loves.'

The whole spectacle was a mixture of formality, pomp, glamour, theatre, reverence – along with genuine affection and love, and the unalloyed happiness of sharing in a young couple's dream come true. On the one hand was the ritual of the National Anthem, heard again and again as royalty arrived, and then sounding for the final time before the service as the bridal coach drew up before the West Door. On the other was the ordinary spectacle of a happy young woman arriving for her wedding. 'Listen to the cheers! And with that great cheer to warm her, she pauses to look at the abbey – perhaps a little nervous in her heart.'

Once again the timing was precise. It was exactly half past eleven when the king and the princess were greeted at the West Door by the massed ranks of the abbey clergy. As *The*

Westminster Abbey

As Westminster Abbey was being prepared for the wedding, temporary lavatories were made available behind the scenes, and both the Chapter House and St George's Chapel were fitted out as retiring rooms for the Gentlemen-At-Arms and the bridesmaids.

The altar was dressed with the Abbey's resplendent gold plate, and flower arrangements were placed on either side of it. Immediately behind the altar, St Edward's Chapel was equipped with the register for the bride, groom and witnesses to sign, along with the gold, quill-shaped pen that was a wedding present to the princess.

The Duke of Edinburgh and his groomsman had entered by the Poet's Corner Door. When the Duke and Duchess left the Abbey by the West Door, their procession skirted the Tomb of the Unknown Soldier which lies in the middle of the nave at the west end. It was here that the Dean of Westminster Abbey later laid the bride's bouquet.

Times described it, the princess, 'looked at once happy and singularly childlike… But the expression in the eyes of the king was that of any father who is filled at once with pride in the daughter he is handing into another's care and with unfeigned delight in the happiness she has found.'

Inside, the royal guests had taken their seats and Vaughan-Thomas was describing the scene to his vast array of listeners all over the world. It was the colour and the grandeur that captivated him: 'this rich pageant of uniform and ecclesiastical finery … the Cross of Westminster with its glitter of ivory and sapphires … the altar, by ancient tradition devoid of flowers but shining with the majestic gold of the abbey plate … the banks of flowers on all sides'.

Fanfares greeted the bride as she moved slowly up the nave on her father's arm. And as she took her place next to the groom, the *Daily Mirror* described the duke as

> self-possessed and calm. For a second he finds the hassock at his feet out of place, so, with a neat left-foot dribble, he centres it beneath him. This calm young man is worth your observation. This is no pale shadow of a consort.

Now the Archbishop of Canterbury, supported by the Archbishop of York and members of the abbey clergy, moved forward to begin the traditional Anglican marriage

service. The form used was a conflation of that laid out in the Book of Common Prayer of 1662 with the alternative order contained in the Deposited Book of 1928. The exchange of vows was in the ancient form, and included the bride's traditional promise to obey her husband. The BBC commentary was minimal, leaving the service to speak for itself, and picking up well the resonant voice of the Archbishop of Canterbury

The Boy Scouts
Association logo.

Peter Townsend

Wing Commander Peter Townsend was Equerry-in-Waiting to the king and took his seat in the third carriage in the procession. He was a highly decorated Battle of Britain pilot who had been the king's equerry since 1944. His later ill-fated love affair with Princess Margaret, who could not marry him because he was divorced, set gossip columns alight in the 1950s.

and the responses of bride and groom – Philip's firm and deep, Elizabeth's lighter and quieter.

Vows made and wedding ring now on the bride's finger, Dr Garbett, Archbishop of York, addressed the newly created husband and wife: 'One of you, the daughter of our much loved king and queen, has gained already by charm and simple grace the good wishes and affection of all; and the other, as a sailor, has a sure place in the hearts of a people who know how much they owe to the strong shield of the Royal Navy.' But their wedding, he went on to say,

> …notwithstanding the splendour and national significance of the service in this Abbey… is an all essentials exactly the same as it would be for any cottager who might be married this afternoon in some small country church in a remote village in the Dales. The same vows are taken; the same prayers are offered; and the same blessings are given…

The 23rd Psalm was then sung to the traditional Crimond, but with 'a charming descant added at the princess's special request', and the service ended with the Archbishop of Canterbury's final blessing and the magnificent Orlando Gibbons 'Amen', followed by a verse of the National Anthem.

The couple then moved into Edward the Confessor's shrine behind the altar, where they signed the register with a gold pen presented to the princess by the Chartered Institute of Secretaries. The Archbishop of Canterbury, the king and queen, Queen Mary and Princess Andrew added their signatures, and further names – those of the bridesmaids, the groomsman and other senior members of the royal family – were inscribed later at Buckingham Palace.

The formalities of the marriage service and the signing of the register were over, and it was time for solemnity to be replaced by happy relaxation and the relieved jolliness into which all weddings tend to develop. As the new Duke and Duchess of Edinburgh left St Edward's Chapel, they paused opposite Queen Mary and, as *The Times* reported,

> made reverence with a curtsey and a deep bow. It was a charming epilogue to a ceremony full of beautiful associations; and then, still walking hand in hand, with joy in their eyes and pride and hope in their mien, they passed down through choir and nave and went out to meet the plaudits of the people.

Back to Buckingham Palace

Trumpet fanfares heralded the start of the procession down the nave, followed by Mendelssohn's traditional *Wedding March*. The bells of Westminster Abbey pealed a welcome as the doors were thrown open and those waiting outside caught their first glimpse of the radiant newlyweds.

Richard Dimbleby commented that it had been a little cold outside the abbey during the service, 'but all that is forgotten now. She steps into the Glass Coach, her train is folded in with her, the Duke of Edinburgh stands waiting, there are smiles on every face. The escort is ready, the horses prancing and bucking, and they are off back to Buckingham Palace past the cheering crowds.'

Slowly the other members of the royal family appeared at the abbey doors, waiting for the coaches and cars that were to take them back to the palace. As the king and queen stepped into the Irish State Coach that had brought the bride to the abbey, 'the anthem is almost drowned out by the noise of the crowd'. The arrangements were faultless as

Corgis

Corgis are small Welsh dogs, descended from dogs introduced to Wales by the Vikings. The name means 'dwarf dog'.

Princess Elizabeth's father was the first member of the royal family to own a corgi, acquired in 1933. Elizabeth's first corgi, Susan, who accompanied her on honeymoon, was an 18th birthday present. Most of the corgis Elizabeth has owned since are Susan's descendants.

The queen usually has at least four corgis as pets, and has also introduced the 'dorgi' – a corgi-dachshund cross – to her household.

the various vehicles left their parking places in Dean's Yard and drew up to the abbey entrance to pick up their passengers. But, as Dimbleby noticed, some among the glittering array of guests were not recognized by the police controlling the crowds: 'The little boy king of Iraq is standing in his blue suit looking at the horses and one of the policemen has beckoned him to come back into the crowd, thinking he's an ordinary young boy who has strayed out of line.'

Meanwhile, in the abbey, Vaughan-Thomas was chronicling the human moments within the solemnity of the ceremonial: 'Her Majesty the Queen smiling across at her daughter; the best man stepping forward to help the pages with the train; the train billowing up behind the bride as she stooped into her deep curtsey to her grandmother'. But now here in the abbey, though the bells were still pealing, the event was winding down: the music was fading, the last organ notes had died away, the choirboys had gone and the guests were standing around, waiting to go, just like at every wedding. As the commentary recorded,

> People are relaxing and chatting: I can see Mr Attlee and Mr Bevin talking to each other, Mr Eden waiting to move, Mr and Mrs Churchill standing nearby. The colour is beginning to fade away – that simple wearing of uniform and vestments that produced for the princess in these austerity days a feast of colour.

Indeed, as Vaughan-Thomas summed it up, 'We will remember for a very long time to come the splendour, dignity and charm of this royal wedding.'

The City of Westminster logo on the City Engineer's letter.

Outside Buckingham Palace, Frank Gillard was once again on air, waiting at the foot of the Victoria Memorial for the carriages and cars to return. The crowd had grown to enormous dimensions while the service in the abbey was going on, and he could see a mass of faces looking down the Mall, waiting for the splendid cavalcade to appear: 'Echoes of cheering can just be heard. And now we see for the first time the bridegroom – up to now we have not seen His Royal Highness the Duke of Edinburgh. The thrill of the emotion is almost physical.'

To the background of horses' hooves, Gillard heralded the arrival of the Glass Coach, 'with the great crowd about to give its welcome to Their Royal Highnesses the bride and bridegroom. The sun has shone though it is now dull, but visibility is clear.' And then he turned his microphone to the crowd, to allow them 'to express their welcome themselves.'

The other processions gradually made their way back down the Mall from Westminster Abbey, and the noise outside the palace became even more deafening as the crowds waited for the royal family to appear on the balcony. It was not long before they got their wish, as the doors opened and the bridal couple stepped out, smiling and waving at the hugely enthusiastic audience (plate 9). Then came the king and queen, Queen Mary, Princess Andrew and Princess Margaret, together with others from the wedding party – a family group, just like any other on the day of a beloved daughter's wedding, but this time symbolic of something more unusual: a country letting its hair down after years of strife and hardship, and just simply enjoying itself (plate 21).

Eventually the royal party left the balcony and went to the Throne Room where the photographer, Baron, took the official photographs. Then they repaired to the Ball Supper Room for the wedding breakfast – a relatively modest meal for just 150 family, courtiers and close friends. The guests were seated at 15 tables, each with a gold vase holding white and pink flowers and with gold plates and cutlery. It was a glorious spectacle, but the meal itself reflected the austerity of the time – just three courses, with partridge chosen as the main dish because it was unrationed. The king's chef had honoured the bride and groom by naming the other two courses after them: Filet de Sole Mountbatten and Bombe Glacée Princess Elizabeth. It was reported that the king apologized to his new son-in-law that the fish course was named Mountbatten rather than Edinburgh; but the menus had been printed the previous week, before the announcement of Philip's new titles and so they had had to use the name he carried at the time.

Crawfie was one of the select number at the wedding breakfast, and later wrote that the speeches were very brief indeed and almost inaudible in that large room without the benefit of microphones. The king, afflicted all his life with a stammer, understandably disliked speech-making and kept his remarks on this occasion to the bare minimum. Both Philip and Elizabeth made short speeches too, according to the press. Philip said 'I am proud – proud of my country and of my wife', while Elizabeth wished for 'nothing more than that Philip and I should be as happy as my father and mother have been, and Queen Mary and King George before them.'

The younger members of the royal family, according to Crawfie, were by this time thoroughly overtired. The two little page boys, in particular, had had a long day of dutiful

The bridal bouquet

The bouquet, by Martin Longman of the Worshipful Company of Gardeners, consisted of white cattleya, odontoglossum and cypripedium orchids. It also had a sprig of myrtle from the bush planted by Prince Albert at Osborne House, which all royal brides since have included in their bouquets. At Elizabeth's request her bouquet was laid on the Tomb of the Unknown Soldier, as her mother had done with hers.

Metropolitan Police logo
used on official letters.

ceremonial and were relieved to be out of the public eye; Prince William of Gloucester reacted, according to eyewitnesses, by charging up and down the palace corridors and having to be restrained from opening the balcony doors and rushing out to see the crowds. They were quickly bundled up in shawls by their nannies and carried off to a quiet part of the palace for a peaceful lunch with the other children, followed by a nap, while the more formal proceedings were going on in the Ball Supper Room.

Departing on honeymoon

Under the headline 'A Day of Smiles' – and after apologizing that the shortage of paper meant that they were unable to print more copies – the *Daily Mirror* of 21 November reported the scenes in the early evening dusk as the bride and bridegroom drove away from Buckingham Palace in an open landau. The crowd had waited untiringly all afternoon and now they were there to witness the traditional sending-off of new husband and wife on their honeymoon. It was getting dark and fog was beginning to descend, but as the gates of the palace forecourt opened, there to be seen were all the close family and friends, with Princess Margaret and the other bridesmaids leading the race to shower the couple with rose petals. As the open landau departed, the king and queen turned back to the palace at the end of an exhausting but supremely happy day; and the queen was heard to remark that she was delighted that the fog had held off.

Once again, crowds lined the streets between the palace and Waterloo Station, with some spectators so eager to see the couple that they perched precariously on the balustrades of the bridge over the River Thames as the landau passed. Elizabeth and Philip were to join at Waterloo the train that would take them to Winchester, in Hampshire, from where a car transported them onwards to Broadlands, Lord Mountbatten's home in Romsey, for the first part of their honeymoon. When they reached Waterloo they were greeted by the stationmaster at platform 11, where a footman carried the bride's fur coat and led her Welsh corgi dog, Susan, to the train.

The bride's going-away outfit, like almost every outfit worn by Elizabeth and her close female family that day, was also by Norman Hartnell. It was described in detail by the fashion writers in the newspapers. There had been some controversy in fashion quarters during the last year, when the celebration of the end of the war in some couture houses had taken the form of over-long designs, using too much scarce fabric. Now, as the press reported, 'The princess has taken her stand in the long-skirt argument – both frock and coat are a little longer than she has been wearing, but still a good 15in from the ground.' The outfit consisted of a dress and coat, in a delicate mid-blue, as well as a felt beret trimmed with an ostrich pompon and two-toned blue ostrich quills; in the usual royal tradition, the hat was designed not to hide her face. Both coat and dress were simply cut and plainly decorated, with the dress falling into three pleats on the left side with a small bow above them.

Cheering crowds saw them off at Waterloo; and cheering crowds awaited their arrival at Winchester station. The huge crowds are indeed one of the defining images of this wedding. It has already been noted how frequently the broadcasters stopped their commentaries and turned their microphones towards the spectators so that listeners could hear and appreciate for themselves the clear enjoyment of those lucky enough to be there. Photographs too, taken from high vantage points along the processional routes in London, show a veritable sea of people everywhere (plate 7), with every window, rooftop and balcony filled to bursting with people straining to see what they could. It seemed that on this day the centre of London was the place to be – merely to be close to the princess's wedding, just to be there and to be part of it, however far away from the action.

And they were well behaved, too. Gillard had reported a surge outside Buckingham Palace as the bride was leaving,

The Royal Honeymoons

Queen Victoria and Albert – Windsor Castle (1840).

Edward VII and Alexandra – Osborne House (1863).

George V and Mary – York Cottage on the Sandringham Estate, a wedding gift from his father (1893).

George VI and Elizabeth– Polesden Lacey, Surrey (1923).

Elizabeth II and Philip – Broadlands, Hampshire, followed by Birkhall on the Balmoral estate (1947).

when the police cordon had been briefly broken, and the debriefings afterwards made it clear that there were several others (pages 99 and 101). But these incursions did not interrupt or disrupt events, and were not caused by bad behaviour – merely by the swayings and surgings inevitable when hundreds of people are crushed together, all trying to see and all taken up with the excitement of the occasion.

As always, children were among the most vulnerable in crowds of this magnitude. There was always a risk of them getting lost or being squashed in the throng. Several press photographs show the familiar sight of young boys and girls being passed over the heads of the crowd to the front (plate 20) after fears had been aroused that they might be over-whelmed by the sheer numbers around them. A debriefing in the National Archives' files includes the report of an incident:

> Opposite the Duke of York steps, as the royal procession was
> passing, [when] a section of the crowd started to sway badly.
> The Police Sergeant endeavoured to control the crowd and
> noticed that two little girls in the centre of the crowd were in
> danger of being crushed. With the assistance of PC Bassett,
> also mounted, he removed the children from the crowd, each
> officer carrying a child on the wallet of his saddle, and taking
> them to the rear of the crowd where they were immediately
> claimed by their parents.   [MEPO 2/7967]

The enthusiasm of the vast crowds went on far into the
evening and night. They were not about to pack up their
vacuum flasks and their sandwich bags, fold up their
waterproofs and groundsheets, and meekly go home once
the public part of the ceremonial was over. Even after the
couple's departure, the throngs outside Buckingham Palace
were indefatigable, shouting and singing, demanding yet
more appearances on the balcony of the bride's family – 'We
want the king'; 'We want the queen'; 'We want Margaret'
– along with impromptu renditions of the National Anthem
and 'For they are jolly good fellas'. It was not until after
11pm, when the king and queen appeared on the balcony
once more, for the fourth and final time, that the crowds
began to depart for home. It was then that the floodlighting
was switched off, and the great day was finally over.

4
NOW WE ARE MARRIED...

The new Duke and Duchess of Edinburgh were to spend the first five nights of their honeymoon at Broadlands, and it must have been a great relief to arrive there finally, after the long and exhausting day. But whereas most honeymooners are able to tell each other what a pleasure it is to be 'alone at last', this was not quite the case for Elizabeth and Philip. They arrived with a detective, a personal footman, the princess's dresser, Bobo, and a valet for the duke – as well as Susan the corgi. Elizabeth had 15 pieces of luggage, Philip had two. They were met at Broadlands by the resident Mountbatten staff, too, and there were rubberneckers outside the gates of the house whom the detective tried to keep at bay. It was not exactly peaceful.

They were both, of course, royal, and used to a world peopled with staff and servants; but if it was normal for Elizabeth to be looked after and waited on intimately at all hours of the day and night, it was less so for Philip. He had led a less closeted and perhaps a less affluent life, having to fend

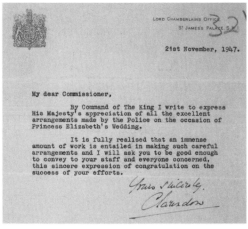

LORD CHAMBERLAINS OFFICE
ST JAMES'S PALACE, S.W.I

21st November, 1947.

My dear Commissioner,

By Command of The King I write to express His Majesty's appreciation of all the excellent arrangements made by the Police on the occasion of Princess Elizabeth's Wedding.

It is fully realised that an immense amount of work is entailed in making such careful arrangements and I will ask you to be good enough to convey to your staff and everyone concerned, this sincere expression of congratulation on the success of your efforts.

Yours sincerely,
Clarendon

The king's thanks to the police.

for himself in many more ways than his wife had ever had to. For her at least, this houseful of people was simply the norm. But in any event, they all – newlyweds and their attendants – were weary. After an early supper Elizabeth and Philip retired to their own room.

But even on honeymoon they could not avoid the outside world. Selected photographers from the press were allowed into the Broadlands grounds on one of their days there to take shots for the ever-hungry newspaper-reading public; and Romsey Abbey was besieged by both the press and the general public on the Sunday following the wedding when they attended a service there. However, the two weeks they then spent at Birkhall, on the Balmoral estate – after briefly returning to London for lunch with the king and queen – were much more peaceful. Life there was comfortable and secluded, and they had a lot more time to themselves to get used to one another and to married life.

After the wedding

On 21 November Major-General Marriott, the military commander in London, wrote to Sir Harold Scott, Commissioner of the Metropolitan Police: 'My dear Sir Harold, you must be a very relieved man today. May I say how perfect the police arrangements were from every point of view, and I do congratulate you on a wonderful piece of organization.'

This was just one of a stream of letters to and from all those who had worked so hard behind the scenes on 20 November to ensure that all went smoothly and seamlessly. In that perhaps more punctilious time, all those involved – palace officials, Ministry of Works staff, Home Office staff, the police, the many other organizations whose help had been necessary on the day – lost no time in thanking and congratulating each other for all their good work. Most of the letters are dated 21 November; there was clearly to be no sitting back, no relaxation on the day after the wedding day, and official business was to be transacted as normal.

Among these thank-you messages were two letters written on 21 November by the Lord Chamberlain, the Earl of Clarendon, to the Right Hon Charles Key MP, the Minister of Works:

> My dear Minister, By command of The King, I am writing to express to you His Majesty's appreciation of the excellent arrangements that were made by the Ministry of Works in

connection with the royal wedding, both inside and outside the abbey. It is fully realized that an immense amount of extra work devolves on the officials concerned in the Ministry on these occasions and it is hoped that you will be good enough to convey to all concerned this sincere expression of congratulation on the success of your efforts. [AE 9012/1]

He also wrote to Key on behalf of the princess, expressing her thanks for the erection and lighting of the banners in front of Buckingham Palace, but particularly for the floodlighting of the palace (plate 22). She was sure that these 'touches of light and gaiety' had contributed to the success of the day.

A telegram from Elizabeth and Philip was sent to the Home Secretary, Chuter Ede, asking him to thank, on their behalf, the members of the police force for their messages of congratulations and to relay their great appreciation of all their hard work on the day (plate 16). Ede passed this message on to the Commissioner of the Met with his own thanks and appreciation: 'Very long hours had to be worked, but throughout the proceedings the police displayed that tact, cheerfulness and efficiency which enable them not only to control the crowd but also to add to everyone's enjoyment on these national occasions.'

Robert Boothby MP wrote to the press to express the view of millions of listeners that the BBC had surpassed itself in its coverage of the wedding. R.F. Conrad from the Press

The show goes on ...

Immediately after the wedding, the princess's outfit was put on display at St James's Palace alongside the 2,500 wedding presents, and the exhibition was opened to the public. Thousands of people visited it in London, and thousands more when some of the display toured the country as a travelling exhibition.

Equally popular was the newsreel footage of the wedding, taken by the BBC and covering the processions between Buckingham Palace and Westminster Abbey, as well as scenes inside the palace after the service. This was shown in cinemas round the country for many weeks after the wedding, and was seen by large numbers of the general public.

Association wrote to the police to congratulate them for 'their magnificent work':

> The calm and coolheaded way in which they handled a very difficult situation is worthy of the highest praise and, at one time in Trafalgar Square opposite Admiralty Arch, when I was caught up in the midst of a seething mass of people I had first hand experience of how the police, by their good humour and capable control, calmed the fears of the people threatened to be crushed by the pressing crowd. [MEPO 2/7967]

Praise indeed from an organization not usually prone to either admiration or approval!

The Commissioner of the Metropolitan Police also wrote to the Ministry of Works to 'convey his warmest thanks for the assistance given by your Ministry in connection with the arrangements necessary for the royal wedding. It was a great help to be able to rely on the readiness and efficiency with which our numerous requests were met and this has undoubtedly contributed largely to the success of the police arrangements.' The headmaster of Westminster School wrote to thank those responsible for the consideration given to his pupils in allowing them a good viewpoint outside the abbey. The public wrote in, too. Mrs E. Richardson, 'an ordinary person up in London to see the wedding', noted 'how considerate, patient and good-tempered the police were on what must have been a very tiring and anxious day.'

The debriefings that started immediately were impressively detailed. Senior police officers and civil servants wanted immediate feedback on what had gone well, what had gone badly and what could be improved next time. All those in command of individual sectors were asked for their comments, their impressions and their recommendations, which were then collated and passed on for future reference.

The United Services Corps helped the police.

Crowd control was a particular issue. One J. Gordon Berry had written to the police deploring the breakdown of police control of the crush on the corner of Trafalgar Square and Whitehall, which had meant that he had had to escort his wife to safety. The reply indicated that they were aware of the incident 'when a section of the crowd got in front of the barrier and police reinforcements had to be deployed to restore the situation' and they duly noted, with thanks, the suggestions he made as to how things might be improved in the future.

On the other hand, Major Anthony Buxton of Horsey Hall, near Great Yarmouth, wrote from his London club, Brooks, to express his appreciation of the police, inspired by Chuter Ede's letter of praise in the *Daily Telegraph*. 'The police, who in addition to showing the greatest efficiency whether mounted or on foot, were really good company and kept everyone smiling'. The major said it was unnecessary to reply, nevertheless a reply was sent. The Commissioner was grateful to receive his letter and wrote 'It has given to all ranks great pleasure to know that their work on that day was so widely appreciated.'

Major films of 1947

The Best Years of Our Lives

Duel in the Sun

The Jolson Story

Forever Amber

Unconquered

Black Narcissus

Brighton Rock

Gentlemen's Agreement – Oscar winner

A Double Life – Oscar winner

Hue and Cry – the first Ealing Comedy

Fame is the Spur

The Farmer's Daughter – Oscar winner

Mourning Becomes Electra

Road to Rio

Miracle on 34th Street – Oscar winner

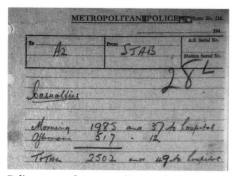

METROPOLITAN POLICE

To A2   From STJAB

Casualties

Morning   1985   and   37   to hospital
Afternoon   517   -   12

Total   2502   and   49   to hospital

Police memo about casualties on the day.

It was agreed that in future more crush barriers would be essential. Other comments were on the lines of 'better arrangements should be made to deal with lost children'; 'it was fortunate that the catering services had been a little ambitious in their provision of food as large numbers of St John's personnel used the canteens as a matter of course'; 'there was inadequate seating available in the canteens for weary officers who had been on their feet for much of the day'. There had been some chaos at the West Door of the abbey after the service when chauffeurs were summoned to pick up their passengers, but found them not there to be picked up when they arrived. Some drivers had circled round and returned up to three times before giving it up as a bad job and simply parking and waiting in the middle of the road.

Overall it seemed to those looking back on the day that arrangements had been excellent, staff and officials had been efficient and that it had all gone well. In some places, it was even felt that they hadn't needed all the police who had been deployed – 'We could have managed with 25% less foot police' – though it was also recommended that in future all senior officers commanding sectors should be mounted.

It was, in fact, the excellent mounted police work outside Buckingham Palace that opened up the route that the landau was due to take on its way to Waterloo Station. When the police found themselves faced with 'thousands of people who were determined not to move', comparatively few horsemen, with the aid of policemen on foot, managed to break up the crowd without undue force in the short space of about 10 minutes. They would have liked a loudspeaker van by the palace gates, but recognized that 'such a move might not have found favour with the palace authorities'.

There were the inevitable glitches. Some of them, it seems, were caused by lack of communication between the police and the military – especially about the routes to be taken by the various units out on duty that day, who were marching between their barracks and their positions. One military band took what was apparently their normal route near the Mall, but their arrival disrupted the police arrangements nearby and it took half an hour before everyone could be got back into their proper positions. Since this had happened only shortly before the first of the processions was due through, there had been a modicum of panic. Another police post found itself inconvenienced by the sudden appearance of the King's Guard 'marching from St James's Palace via Stable

Yard which was closed. It would have been more suitable had the Guard used Marlborough Yard which was kept open.'

It was also clear that the administrators and planners were not yet at all sure about how to cater for the BBC. These days, broadcasting and press organizations are the first to be considered when big public events are being planned, and can also usually insist on the logistics of their needs being given priority – even to the extent of the timing of the event being arranged around their peak periods. In 1947 there was no such understanding. It has already been noted that the broadcasters within Westminster Abbey found themselves having to share the triforium with numbers of palace staff who had been allocated tickets there to watch the service. It seems that a similar situation had arisen on the roof of Admiralty Arch on the wedding day, and that there had been some tension between BBC staff working there and others who had been allowed access. Meetings were now being held to ensure that such problems would be less likely to arise in future.

Worldwide rejoicing

The wedding had been broadcast to an audience accross the world. Dr Garbett, the Archbishop of York, acknowledged as much in his address to the new Duke and Duchess of Edinburgh after they had exchanged their vows:

In the presence of this congregation and in the hearing of an invisible audience in all parts of the world you have now become man and wife. Never before has a wedding been followed with such interest by so many, and this has not been merely passive; it has been accompanied by the heartfelt prayer and good wishes of millions, and hope that throughout your married life you may have every happiness and joy.

The City of London Police logo.

The announcer at the start of the radio coverage had catalogued the stations all over the world that were covering the wedding; not just the BBC's home, overseas and European stations, but also those in 50 Commonwealth countries, the USA networks and independent stations, the networks of most European countries and those serving the British forces abroad. They were all there to 'share in this day of rejoicing for the British Commonwealth of Nations.'

Dr Garbett's belief that the good wishes of millions were with the couple was echoed in the coverage given by *The Times* of 21 November to the way in which the people of countries across the world had followed the broadcasts.

From Canada it was observed that 'Ottawans, mostly in family groups, rose at 5.45am to tune into the ceremony and its attendant celebrations, and thousands of Canadians all across the country … felt themselves to to be in kinship with the cheering throngs assembled between Buckingham Palace and Westminster Abbey.'

New York commentators remarked on how 'American newspapers today published many columns of description and pictures of Princess Elizabeth's wedding, and great numbers of people, in further evidence of the eager interest that there is in this country in a truly romantic royal marriage, rose hours earlier than usual to listen to broadcast accounts of the ceremony and the pageantry surrounding it.'

The royal wedding attracted Australia's greatest radio audience as stations broadcast descriptions of it for nearly three hours: 'No occasion since Victory Day has captured the fancy of and stirred the public to such enthusiasm as Princess Elizabeth's wedding. Australians were determined to share in Britain's rejoicing and, though thousands of miles separated them from the scene, they were brought into almost intimate touch with the proceedings by the wireless.'

In South Africa, where Elizabeth had spent time with her family before announcing her engagement, there was no public holiday, but normal work patterns slowed as people listened to the royal wedding broadcast from London, relayed by local stations: 'Crowds gathered outside shops where loudspeakers were installed and in many places whole staffs gathered round portable radios.'

The royal wedding was a gala occasion in Malaysia where

it was celebrated with parades and processions. *The Times* reported that 'Special services were held in the Muslim mosques, Buddhist temples and Christian churches. In Singapore the army and RAF gave a display, and the Chinese community had a huge lantern procession.'

French newspapers had been the first to hint at Elizabeth's engagement, and for the French people the wedding was the 'event of the day'. In a country also reconstructing after the war, electricity cuts were suspended so that millions could listen to the broadcast of the abbey service transmitted by 19 of the 40 wireless stations across the country. *The Times* correspondent wrote that 'the innumerable enquiries received, the space devoted to descriptions and photographs of the ceremony in all the evening newspapers, even the Communist *Ce Soir*, bear witness to feelings in this country.'

All of which goes to endorse in no half measure Peter Scott's pronouncement outside Westminster Abbey, as Princess Elizabeth was driven up to her wedding, that 'she is our princess'. And now she was embarking on her new adventure.

Married life

It is slightly odd to recall that, like many newlywed couples, the Duke and Duchess of Edinburgh did not have a home of their own when they were first married. The country house that was to have been theirs, in Sunninghill Park, burnt down in the middle of 1947 before they could move in, and Clarence House, which was assigned to them as their central London home, was in dire need of refurbishment. So for the first 18 months of their life together, Elizabeth and Philip spent most of the time living with the bride's parents at one or other of the royal residences, interspersed with rented or borrowed accommodation. It was not until May 1949 that they could finally take possession of Clarence House.

The duke was – and wished to be – still in the Royal Navy and soon started a desk job at the Admiralty. But the royal 'family firm' was a small one, and he quickly found himself combining his naval career with royal duties, which his wife was also carrying out on a large scale. Their first official trip abroad as a couple was in May 1948, when they spent four days in Paris on a goodwill mission to the French government and people which was a huge success. The beautiful young princess and her handsome husband were feted wherever they went, with the sort of crowds following them around that were to become familiar again, with the advent of another princess, some 30 years later.

Philip's naval career was to blossom, and included a lengthy posting in Malta, starting in the autumn of 1949, where Elizabeth joined him for several weeks at a time and where, it is said, they were able to lead a much more 'normal' life than was possible amidst the formalities of royal life in

London. But the king's health was failing, and they found themselves increasingly undertaking the foreign trips that he could no longer manage. And it was not to be long before her father's death on 6 February 1952 catapulted Elizabeth into the role she had hoped to avoid for many years yet, and ended Philip's hopes of continuing his naval life.

But meanwhile they had become parents. Their first child, Charles, was born on 14 November 1948. The official announcement went up on the railings of Buckingham Palace just after 11pm that evening:

> Her Royal Highness the Princess Elizabeth, Duchess of Edinburgh, was safely delivered of a Prince at 9.14 o'clock this evening. Her Royal Highness and the infant Prince are both doing well.

They then had a daughter, Anne, born on 15 August 1950, and were later to have two more sons, Andrew and Edward.

The fairytale that had started on that cold, grey November day in 1947 seemed to have come to its natural fruition. The early death of Elizabeth's much loved father had changed both their lives immeasurably, and cut short what they must have hoped would be several years of a much lower-profile life. But their marriage has proved strong and enduring, a fact commemorated in the celebration of their Diamond Jubilee on 20 November 2007.

The motto translates as 'God and my right'.

Acknowledgements

The original material cited here comes from the Metropolitan Police, Home Office, Ministry of Works and Foreign Office documents held by the National Archives. The main files are:

MEPO 2/7967: Metropolitan Police correspondence

AE 9012/1: Ministry of Works correspondence

ADM 178/389: Private Office file 27198/1946 – Philip's naturalization

CAB 134/215 and 195/5: Cabinet discussions of Civil List

FO 372: messages of congratulations and diplomatic concerns

HO 144/23364: Home Office correspondence

The British Library holds BBC broadcasts of the wedding service and the processions available on discs: LP 11015, LP11018, LP 11024, MP 11081, 11984, and the relevant newspapers of the time.

Books

Gyles Brandreth *Philip and Elizabeth: Portrait of a Marriage* (Century, 2004)

Marion Crawford *The Little Princesses* (Cassell, 1952).

Five Gold Rings: A Royal Wedding Souvenir Album from Queen Victoria to Queen Elizabeth II (Royal Collection Publications, 2007)

Websites

www.dandantheweatherman.com

www.fortunecity.co.uk

www.royal.co.uk

Picture acknowledgements

The Publishers would like to thank the following for permission to use images in this book: Hulton Archive/Getty Images, **1**, **4**, **9**, **14**, **18**, **25**, front and back cover; Mirrorpix **13**, **21**; UPPA/Photoshot **24**. All other images are from The National Archives' documents as described above.

Index